The **CHEESES** *of*
CALIFORNIA

The CHEESES of CALIFORNIA

A CULINARY TRAVEL GUIDE

JEANETTE HURT

THE COUNTRYMAN PRESS
WOODSTOCK, VERMONT

ISBN 978-0-88150-812-3

Cover photo © California Milk Advisory Board
Interior photos by the author unless otherwise specified
Book design and composition by Eugenie Delaney
Maps by Paul Woodward © The Countryman Press

Published by The Countryman Press, P.O. Box 748,
Woodstock, Vermont 05091

Distributed by W. W. Norton & Company, Inc.,
500 Fifth Avenue, New York, NY 10110

Printed in the United States of America

10 9 8 7 6 5 4 3 2 1

DEDICATION

This book is dedicated to my in-laws: Jeanne and Ed Potter,

Craig Edwards and Sarah (Sally) Dowhower, and Marcie Hutton.

It is also dedicated to my super nephews, Eric and Ryan Hutton, who LOVE cheese.

ACKNOWLEDGMENTS

This book could not have been written without the assistance of so many people, and I may be remiss in thanking some of you, for which I apologize in advance. I owe a great deal of gratitude to all of the wonderful folks at the California Milk Advisory Board, especially Tricia Heinrich. Special thanks also go out to the California Artisan Cheese Guild and Lynne Devereaux. I also need to thank Gordon Edgar, Barrie Lynn, Gretchen Roberts, and Sheana Davis for their assistance. It also would not have been possible if Steve Ehlers and Patty Peterson (and Larry, too) hadn't introduced me to Cowgirl Creamery's Red Hawk and Cypress Grove's Humboldt Fog not so many years ago—thanks for keeping me well stocked in cheese. Special thanks go out to all of the wonderful people who helped me arrange my trips to California: Tami Von Isakovics and Ashley Rodgers of Wagstaff Worldwide; Beth Costa of the Russian River Wine Road; Nancy Uber of NÜ PR; Debbie Geiger of Geiger PR; Richard Stenger and Tony Smithers of the Humboldt County CVB; Mark Carter, Lowell Daniels and Jenny Oaks, and Ron and Cosette Scheiber. I owe a debt of gratitude to my dear friends Stephen Magyari and his partner, Dr. Eric Nicely, and to my friends Kristi Murphy and her husband, Jeff Kroke, who gave me insiders' tips, views, and a place to crash. A warm thank you goes out to Bob and Martha Haynes, brother and sister-in-law of my dear (adopted) grandparents, Dick and Ellen Haynes, whose loving support was so welcome. Gratitude is owed to my entire editorial team: Kermit Hummel, Kim Grant, Jennifer Thompson, Lisa Sacks, Courtney Andree, and Sandy Rodgers; thanks for making my words sound even better. Lastly, I have to thank my family: my wonderful and supportive husband, Kyle; my parents, Tom and Mary Hurt; and my sisters, Julie and Karen Hurt. Special thanks go out to my dear mother, again, for her tireless work at helping me index this volume. I also could not have a more supportive extended family: the Rudniks (also Neubauers), the Nevens (Sheldons, Cornings, and Porembas, too), the Hurts (Wongs and

Burkhardts, too), and the Vuyks. Thanks also go out to my friend and Webmaster, Bec Loss, and to my friends Damon Brown, Jen Fichtel, Susan Ward, Krissie Kierzek Acevedo, Marie Dries, Shannon Lucky, Monica Gotomo, Tamara Johnston, Karen Mahliot, Kristine Hansen, Julie Neubauer, and the rest of the gang, for keeping me on track. Thanks also to the wonderful women at my Ignatian Prayer Group—your prayers, encouragement, and support worked wonders! Lastly, this goes out to all the chefs, sommeliers, winemakers, cheese experts, and foodies who took the time to answer my many questions, but most of all, heartfelt thanks go out to the amazing cheesemakers who invited me into their lives and their world. This is for you.

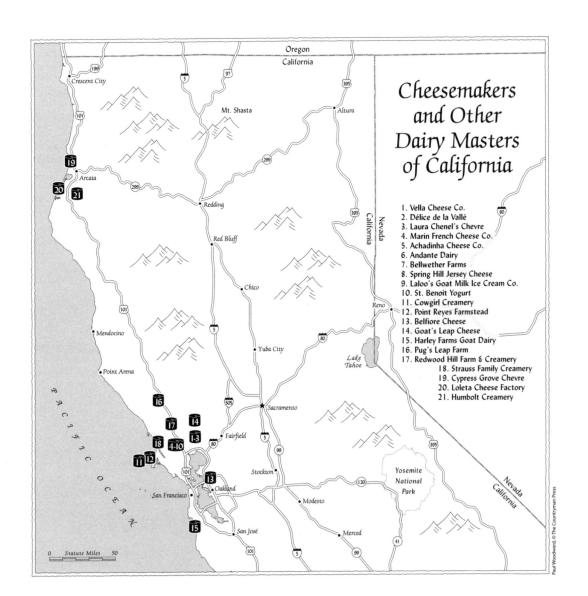

Cheesemakers
and Other
Dairy Masters
of California

1. Vella Cheese Co.
2. Délice de la Vallé
3. Laura Chenel's Chevre
4. Marin French Cheese Co.
5. Achadinha Cheese Co.
6. Andante Dairy
7. Bellwether Farms
8. Spring Hill Jersey Cheese
9. Laloo's Goat Milk Ice Cream Co.
10. St. Benoit Yogurt
11. Cowgirl Creamery
12. Point Reyes Farmstead
13. Belfiore Cheese
14. Goat's Leap Cheese
15. Harley Farms Goat Dairy
16. Pug's Leap Farm
17. Redwood Hill Farm & Creamery
18. Strauss Family Creamery
19. Cypress Grove Chevre
20. Loleta Cheese Factory
21. Humbolt Creamery

Paul Woodward, © The Countryman Press

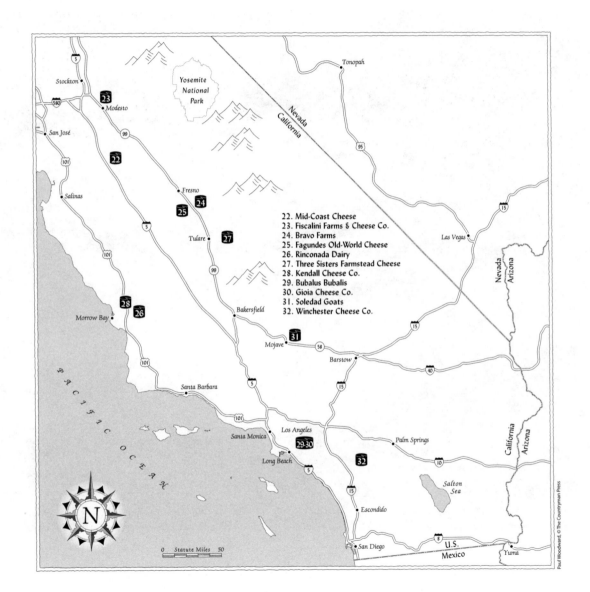

22. Mid-Coast Cheese
23. Fiscalini Farms & Cheese Co.
24. Bravo Farms
25. Fagundes Old-World Cheese
26. Rinconada Dairy
27. Three Sisters Farmstead Cheese
28. Kendall Cheese Co.
29. Bubalus Bubalis
30. Gioia Cheese Co.
31. Soledad Goats
32. Winchester Cheese Co.

Paul Woodward, © The Countryman Press

CONTENTS

APPENDIXES

INTRODUCTION

"Many's the long night I've dreamed of cheese—toasted, mostly."
—ROBERT LOUIS STEVENSON

I have a thing for cheese. Some might call it a problem of sorts, a mild addiction if you will. I blame it on my heritage. I am the granddaughter of a Wisconsin dairy farmer, and I am the grandniece of a New York dairy farmer. And I recently learned that my great-uncle Raymond G. Rudnik invented—and patented—the mechanization and the machine for slicing and packaging processed cheese. He used to work at Kraft, and he may also have been the inventor of those little jelly packages you find in diners everywhere, but that could have been a distant cousin.

So, dear reader, you might be asking yourself what am I, with deep dairy roots east of the Mississippi, doing writing a book about California cheese? The answer is really rather simple. I love good cheese, and I can't swear allegiance to only eat cheese made by the state in which my car is registered. I admit I do like to eat local, but that rule goes out the window when it comes to foods like pineapples and Roquefort. Same goes for Dry Jack and Red Hawk. Point Reyes blue and Fiscalini bandaged cheddar. Humboldt Fog and Délice de la Vallée.

I also happen to be someone who, instead of taking home souvenirs when she travels, takes home recipes and foods. And when I return home, I track down such delicacies with a vengeance—either at my favorite gourmet store, Larry's Market—or via the amazing wonder of the Internet. I am so grateful that I can find many of California's lovely dairy beauties so far from their home.

I'm a sucker for great cheese, and after traveling across California, sampling the work of happy cows—as well as happy goats and even happy water buffaloes—I can honestly say I adore California cheese. Yes, California is a big state, and it's home to big, big dairy herds, but its grandness, I think, can best be measured by the little artisans who craft an even bigger bang of taste. As California has long been the leader in the country's natural foods movement, it naturally has amazing organic, local, and quite "green" cheeses.

Come join me on this journey of cheese greatness. By the time you've finished reading this book, I bet you'll be as addicted as I am. But you can't blame it on your genes. I, on the other hand, have a perfectly good excuse as to why my refrigerator currently has about 5 pounds of the luscious stuff sitting where my vegetables used to be.

CHAPTER 1

How California Has Become the
CHEESE LEADER

*A*ny oenophiles worth their wine bottle collections should be able to tell you about 1976's "Judgment of Paris." Heck, anyone who's seen the movie *Bottle Shock* should be able to detail the basics of this phenomenal story; of how the world reacted in awe and wonder when California wines beat the pants off the French stalwarts in a blind taste testing.

But probably not as many cheese lovers will be able to tell you about 2007's "Judgment of London," and how California cheese took on—and then took out—both the French and the British wheels with one quick swipe of the trier. Now, that story would also make a great movie—and if any California filmmakers want to make a flick about this fabulous, international incident, I would suggest they call it *Culture Shock*. But even if it never gets told on the big screen, it's worth more than a mention, and it really illustrates how incredible California cheese is.

Let me tell you about it. The World Cheese Awards is where it starts out. Organized by the Guild of Fine Foods in the United Kingdom, the competition is part of the Taste of London Show, and it's been held for more than 20 years. Every year up to 2,000 different cheeses are judged, and these cheeses hail from, well, all over the world. As one of the most prestigious cheese contests and probably *the* cheese competition to win in Europe, winning isn't easy, and cheesemakers send in their best efforts to be critiqued by a panel of international judges.

Just as there were two California wines involved in the Judgment of Paris, there were two California cheeses critiqued in the Judgment of London. Fiscalini Cheese's 18-month-old bandaged cheddar, handcrafted by expert cheesemaker Mariano Gonzales, won the Wyke Farms Trophy for "best extra mature traditional cheese." It was the first non-British cheese ever to win that award.

The second California cheese company to wrest away an award from the Europeans was Marin French Cheese Company, which in the same competition won gold in the Brie category. Interestingly enough, this was the second gold for Marin French's Brie; they first dominated the French in the 2005 competition.

But unlike the Judgment of Paris, which was a singular sort of contest that pitted the French wines against the California wines directly, the Judgment of London was a more happenstance domination. "That competition was an ambush," says Jim Boyce, owner of Marin French, of the Parisian event. "The World Cheese Awards is an upfront contest, with one hundred twenty judges."

Wheels of San Joaquin Gold rest in the aging room of Fiscalini Cheese.

While the Judgment of Paris immediately had reverberations in the wine world, the Judgment of London happened rather quietly, at least where the American media were concerned. French newspapers, however, wrote extensively of Marin French's big wins. "This, for California cheese, is very much like it was thirty years ago for California wines," Boyce says.

Which means that it's an exciting time to be involved in California cheese. The World Cheese Awards isn't the only cheese contest where California shows off its skills—it regularly takes home dozens of awards from the American Cheese Society contest, the World Cheese Championship, and the U.S. Cheese Championship. Though the awards are nice, they just give evidence to the truth—California's Real Cheese is really good.

Marin French Cheese Company's bevy of bloomy rinds and their bounty of awards.

And actually it's been quite good for centuries; in fact, California has a long history as a dairy state. Such heritage goes back to 1769 when Father Junípero Serra first started setting up missions, 21 in all, along California's coast. Serra, a Spanish priest, not only set up the missions, he also introduced the first grapes to the region, and as such, he's considered the "Father of California Wine." He could be considered the padre of cheese, as well, because he also brought along the first dairy cattle for cheesemaking.

Cheesemaking expanded beyond the missions in the 1850s when a little something called the Gold Rush happened. Miners came in droves, equipped not only with pans for gold, but also buckets for milk, as they often towed cows behind their wagons. Then, a pioneer woman named Clara Steele came along. She's often credited with starting the first commercial dairy in the United States, as she set it up in Point Reyes in 1857. She made cheese using her grandmother's recipes, and by 1861 she and her family were making 45 tons of cheese a year. Other cheesemaking operations followed, and a distinctly new, American original cheese evolved.

Jim Boyce shows off some of his lovely Bries.

But while the cheese, Monterey Jack, is quite distinct, its origins aren't so exact. It is thought to be a descendant, of sorts, of the original cheeses that Franciscan friars made in the missions, but who and how it was created isn't so concrete. Some say Doña Juana Cota de Boronda created the cheese, which was called at the time *Queso del Pais* (in Spanish it means "Cheese from the Country"), and she sold it door-to-door to fend for her family of 17 after her husband was crippled. Others say Domingo Pedrazzi of Carmel Valley made the cheese using a house jack or a press. But most likely, if it wasn't created by Pedrazzi or Boronda, it got its name from a Monterey entrepreneur named David Jacks, who sold *Queso del Pais* cheese as "Jacks' Cheese" in 1882, and later people asked for Monterey Jack cheese.

Another American original cheese had its start in California—Dry Jack—and it actually is one of those delicious mistakes that forever changes the order of things. In 1915, San Francisco cheese wholesaler D. F. DeBarnardi simply left an order of fresh Monterey Jack in storage for a bit too long. But after tasting it, he discovered that the cheese had acquired a tasty nutty flavor. It grew in popularity when World War I interrupted shipments of aged Italian cheeses, as it makes a great substitute for those grating cheeses.

From the early 1930s to about the year 1970, cheesemaking and dairy-ranching operations hovered at around 16 million pounds. Then things changed dramatically. In 1970, cheese production hovered at about 17.5 million pounds; by 1978 it had grown to a whopping 137 million pounds, and two decades later, in 1993, California eclipsed Wisconsin to become the largest milk producer in the country.

From 1978 until the present, almost every year new dairy production records are set. In 2007, California's dairy business generated $61.4 billion worth of economic activity, setting a record of 41 billion pounds of milk, which represents nearly a 12 percent increase in production just since 2004. Cheese production increased to 2.3 billion pounds in 2007, up 15 percent since 2004, and keeping California's production only second to Wisconsin in overall cheese production. And most dairy experts say it's only a matter of time before California takes over Wisconsin's place in cheese production. "It's not a question of if, it's a question of when," says John Fagundes, master cheesemaker and third-generation California dairyman at Fagundes Farmstead Old World Cheese.

But although the state's 55-plus cheesemakers make more than 250 different varieties of cheese, and make more than a quarter of the country's cheese, and make more mozzarella and Hispanic- or Latino-style cheeses than any other state in the nation, the *big* in California cheese is not just in production amounts. Nor is it simply in the awards that these cheesemakers rack up.

It's big as in big taste, made by little artisan operators. Some of these artisans are like Marin French Cheese Company, which got its start more than 105 years ago, or Vella Cheese Company, which has been churning out small but stellar productions of Monterey Jack and Dry Jack cheese since 1931. They were artisans before artisan

Some happy California goats munch on pasture.

Marin French cows frolic in bucolic Marin County.

cheese was even coined as a term. "There's always been some tradition of really high-quality cheese," says Gordon Edgar, cheese buyer for Rainbow Grocery Cooperative in San Francisco.

And then there are the pioneers in goat's milk cheeses: Laura Chenel, Jennifer Bice, Mary Keehn, and Sadie Kendall. These California women all started raising goats in the 1970s. Laura Chenel, of course, is the first to transform her cheese-making hobby into a commercial business, and after studying the intricacies of chèvre in France, she started making it to sell in 1979. Chef Alice Waters discovered Laura's cheese and, it could be said, that was the start of the artisan cheesemaking movement in California. "There were people doing these kinds of things in the 1970s, and at some point in the early 90s, goat cheese started taking off a bit more," Gordon says. "There was a critical mass. Nationally distributed goat's milk products were not something you could have fathomed in 1970."

Many of these cheesemakers were not only pioneers in California, but also in the overall artisan cheese movement in America. "When we started at the American Cheese Society, there were questions of what is it going to do for me," says Mary, founder and president of Cypress Grove Chèvre.

The American Cheese Society, or ACS as it is known, is perhaps the biggest supporter of artisan cheesemakers in the country, supporting and fostering fine cheesemaking and promoting such cheeses to the public. "But it didn't exist when we were all starting," Mary says.

"Even though everyone was so busy and you couldn't interact (with other cheesemakers) as much, you kind of saw them out of the corner of your eye," says Sadie, founder of Kendall Cheese Company. "They're doing it so maybe we can do it, too."

Farmers' markets and the local food movement (which actually started in Marin County) also helped connect artisans with each other and with consumers. "People started making connections between people who were making cheese and what was sitting mysteriously on a

Holstein cows soak up the sun.

grocery store shelf," Gordon says. "That's really helped popularize small-scale production of cheese throughout the country, and there's a vast difference between a handmade product and a commodity-produced product."

Today's artisan cheesemakers in California range from those working with a handful of goats to those with thousands of cows, but what they all have in common is their quality. That quality is supported by the California Milk Advisory Board (CMAB), which created the Real California Milk seal in 2007, and also created the Real California Cheese seal in the late 1990s. But beyond the CMAB's work at promoting artisan cow's milk cheeses, what's telling is that in 2005 the California Artisan Cheese Guild was founded. The guild supports not just cow's milk cheesemakers, but also makers of goat's milk, sheep's milk, and even water buffalo's milk cheeses, too. "It seems like suddenly, people are just getting bitten by the cheese bug," Mary says. "And as for the future, I don't see people going back."

California isn't going back, in the least. And what is especially interesting to note is that as it goes forward, a curious evolution is occurring. Just as some famous French winemakers have taken to purchasing California vintners—most recently, California's Chateau Montelena, of Judgment of Paris fame, was sold to Cos d'Estournel—some famous California cheese factories have been sold to French companies. Laura Chenel sold her creamery to noted chèvre company Rians. Not only that, but some great European cheesemakers have moved their operations here. Carol and Julian Pierce, who had an award-winning goat's milk creamery in Great Britain, just opened up shop outside Los Angeles. So now their World Cheese Award–winning chèvre is produced in California.

As I write this, I've received word of a couple creameries that might come online with production by 2009, and either one of them has the potential to take on the country, if not the world.

CHAPTER 2

How to Make Cheese,
CALIFORNIA
STYLE

Great cheese starts with great milk. As any good cheesemaker will tell you, it's possible to make bad cheese out of good milk, but it's impossible to make good cheese out of bad milk.

A funny series of commercials brings this point home. They show some bovines moving from a shivering, snowy region to sunny California. Their clever tag line sticks in your brain: "Great cheese comes from happy cows. Happy cows come from California."

California is certainly a land of many happy cows. At last count, in 2007, they numbered 1.8 million, making their homes at 1,960 dairies across the state. That's a rather dramatic increase in just a few years, as their population numbered only 88,000 in 2004. Many of them live on big dairies, with the average herd size in California about 800. But the super-huge herds can number anywhere from 1,000 to 2,000 cattle, to as many as 5,000 or more.

Whereas California may be the land of big herds, not every dairyman or woman boasts herds that large, and indeed, there still are herds of 200 and smaller, too. California may have

MARIN FRENCH CHEESE CO.

A happy Jersey (the breed, not the state) relaxes.

the country's biggest cheese plant, but it also is home to some of the tiniest factories. While it could be said that there is some tension that exists between the large producers and the small ones, they each have carved out their own distinct niches, and their quality speaks for itself. It's also interesting to note that some large dairy farms have small artisan cheesemaking operations, and some small artisan producers actually buy their milk from larger producers, so size isn't always the indicator of quality as one might think. I personally think great cheese comes from great milk, and there is more than one way to go about achieving this.

The great milk in California isn't just from happy cows. California also has happy goats, happy sheep, and even happy water buffalo (and from pictures, the water buffaloes wallowing in water look the happiest to me). That adds even more to the diversity of cheese.

On farmstead cheesemaking operations, the milk is either pumped or carried by hand to the production facilities on site. There, if it is a fresh or bloomy-rind cheese, it will be pasteurized. But if it is a raw milk cheese, it will go straight into the cheesemaking room. The setup varies by cheese type and by individual cheesemaker's desires. "The relationship between a cheesemaker and where they get their milk is critical," says Lynne Devereux, president of the California Artisan Cheese Guild.

Most cheesemakers who do not produce their own milk handpick their sources for milk, and for those who have been making cheese for a while, chances are they've been getting their milk from the same source or sources for a long time, too.

The milk will have a different taste if it is from organically grown livestock, and California has a lot of organic milk producers. But the milk will also have other differences if the cows (or other animals) were pasture grazed. There are two primary types of farms: Those that use rotational grazing techniques and those that feed their livestock traditional, or silage, grain or hay. Rotational, pasture-grazed animals are moved to a different pasture every 12 hours or so. In California, those who pasture graze their animals actually can let them graze for more of the year than is possible in most other states. "I tell people that there are three distinct types of milk throughout the year," says Bob Laffranchi, owner of Loleta Cheese Company. "The big change is in the spring when we go to grass. Then, come May fifteenth, the sun is longer, and we start getting the best milk. Then, the third time is when we get our first cold snap, and we have to be careful that the cheese doesn't get too soft. We adjust our make procedures around those times. At some point, I will have some seasonal cheeses that bring out the milk's best characteristics at each time of the year."

It's not just the time of year that can affect the milk—it is where the animals are grazed or even where the feed is raised that makes a difference. California's largess comes not just from plentiful production or varieties of milk or even varieties of animals—it comes from its vast geographical differences or *terroirs*. *Terroir*, or the French term to describe how geography affects food products, is not just for California's grapes or wines. In fact, it could be said that the *terroir* variety in California is even bigger for milk than it is for wine, as the cheesemaking regions in California cover a greater area. They start practically at the bor-

TOP: *An organic Holstein grazing.*
BOTTOM: *The giant redwoods of Northern California are near the pastures of Humboldt County.*

STRAUS CREAMERY

13

der with Oregon and head all the way south, almost to the border of Mexico. Some cheeses in California are salt-kissed by the Pacific Ocean. Others are crafted in the heat of the desert. And some offer the taste of the greenest pastures.

The Central Valley and the Chino Basin are the state's largest dairy regions, accounting for 8 of the 11 dairy-producing counties, according to the 1997 Census of Agriculture. This is where the larger dairies tend to be located, and this particular *terroir* can be described as warm or hot; the cows are typically fed diets that include fruits and vegetables from the state, including citrus, and on especially heat-filled days, the cows are kept cool by large fans. The farther south and west you go, the hotter the weather tends to get, and that affects the milk.

In northern California the largest concentration of smaller creameries tends to be centered in Sonoma and Marin counties, just north of San Francisco, in the same area where there is also a thriving wine industry. Sonoma County is second only to Napa in terms of overall wine production, and it makes vintages that are just as good or sometimes better, though not as well known, as Napa's bounty. The cows and goats in this *terroir* often graze or browse on hillsides where the fog from the Pacific Ocean rolls in.

It only gets greener and foggier the farther north you go, and in Humboldt County you'll find some of the greenest pastures in all of California. This land of the stately redwood forests—and legendary home to Bigfoot—boasts a long history of dairy, and the cows and goats in this region

Sheep at Rinconada Dairy wait for their dinner.

tend to be pasture grazed; they also are affected by the fog that rolls in from the bay. "We're Baja Oregon," says Bob Laffranchi.

Though the location impacts the cheese, the basic process of cheesemaking remains the same. That process starts out as soon as milk is unloaded at the creamery or as soon as it is milked at a farm. From there it is either transferred to holding tanks or to vats for pasteurization, or if using raw milk, for cheesemaking. Once pasteurized, bacterial cultures are added to start the process. Different cultures produce different cheeses. Cheddars, for example, use a mesophyllic culture, while blue cheeses use a *Penicillium roqueforti* culture. But each cheesemaker has his or her own, usually secret, formula of cultures. In a sense, cheesemaking can be compared to the alchemy of cooking, and a good cheesemaker will know how to use the cultures to get exactly the desired result. Though some cheesemakers make European styles of cheese, their work is uniquely their own.

A *Marin French cheesemaker measures out cultures.*

Pascal Destandau, cheesemaker of Pug's Leap Farm, for example, makes some of the loveliest bloomy rind goat's milk cheeses from milk that partner and co-owner, Eric Smith, garners from their small herd; one bite of his cheeses will transport the taster to the Loire Valley of France. But Pascal doesn't make cheeses exactly the way they do in France, because there cheesemakers use raw milk, and here, under United States guidelines, cheesemakers who don't age their cheeses for 60 or more days cannot use raw milk. Legally, only raw milk cheeses that are aged for more than two months can be sold here. Though Pascal would like to see such laws change, in the meantime he must compensate with his own, unique formulas of cultures and methods of crafting cheese.

Christine Maguire feeds her pigs leftover whey from her farmstead cheesemaking operations.

After cheese cultures do their work—and that usually takes about 45 minutes—then rennet is added. This ingredient coagulates the cheese. Rennet originally came from calves' or goats' stomachs. Today, most cheeses do not use this type of rennet; they're made with a microbial form. Some cheesemakers, like Pascal, however, prefer not to use microbial forms because they are genetically modified.

Rennet is stirred into the milk, usually, but not always, with automatic paddles that go back and forth across the vat. For orange cheddar cheeses, annatto, a plant extract, is added at this point. But more and more cheddars do not have this coloring.

After a time the milk sets, and the cheese looks and feels like a Jell-O salad (some of the most hideous forms of which are immortalized in the book *The Gallery of Regrettable Food*), minus the statuesque forms and the additions of olives or carrots. After the cheese is set, the curds are cut. Cutting the cheese, despite being a euphemism for the passing of gaseous substances, does not emit gases of any sort, but it does allow the curds to separate from the whey. And yes, it is believed that Miss Muffet was eating some form of this until the spider came along. Cheesemakers often cut cheese using cheese harps, large metal paddles that are strung with linear blades.

Whey used to be considered waste and for many years it has been fed to hogs, which is exactly what Christine and Jim Maguire do with their leftover whey at Rinconada Dairy. Their happy, healthy hogs, incidentally, are a much sought-after commodity by local chefs. Christine also uses the whey to wash the rind of one of her cheeses, La Panza Gold. Mozzarella makers, of both the cow and buffalo milk varieties, traditionally use the whey to produce ricotta, and cheesemakers both here in California and in Italy do the same. But today, excluding makers of Italian cheeses, most whey is sold off as a commodity. California, being the largest milk producer in the country, is also the largest producer of whey, and whey gets added into everything from protein drinks to thickeners.

Cheesemakers pour the curds into pails.

From this point on the cheesemaking process changes according to the type of cheese. Many cheeses are poured or pressed into cheese molds. Others, like Monterey Jack, often get washed with water at some point during the process. Cheddar, however, has a distinct process that begins at this point: When the curds begin to stick together, the cheesemaker draws a line down the center of the make table, and then the curds are cut and piled upon one another. Eventually, these curds form slabs, and then the slabs are piled upon each other and

After the curds are poured, they sit so the whey can drain out.

turned several times, about every 15 minutes. This process, which is called cheddaring, presses the curds closer together while even more whey drains out. When it is finished, the slabs are about 1 inch in thickness. Then they are recut into curds and salted.

Salt is an important part of the cheesemaking process. It gives cheese flavor, but it also acts as a natural preservative and it slows down the work of the bacterial cultures. For ched-dar and Monterey Jack cheese, the salt is added in a dry salt method—basically, it's sprinkled into the curds. Other cheeses are soaked in salt brines to absorb the salt, and still others are dry rubbed, or the salt is rubbed directly onto the rind of the cheese.

At this stage, if it is a flavored cheese, the flavors are also added. "California has a long history of flavored cheeses," says Lynne Devereux. Monterey Jacks, cheddars, chèvres, and even Goudas have flavors added. Flavors can be created with garlic, onions, herbs, jalapeño or chipotle chiles, and even smoked salmon.

From this point the curds, and flavors, if they're used, are poured into molds, or stain-less steel hoops or forms. Sometimes the curds of some goat's milk cheesemakers are frozen, because it is harder to maintain consistent goat's milk production year-round. Some cheesemakers say this makes the fresh chèvre taste differently; others say it doesn't affect the taste. It's important to note that while chèvre curds can be frozen, cow's milk curds cannot be frozen because they have a dif-ferent protein structure.

Fresh mozzarella is created through a special process called pasta *filata*. After the curds are formed, the curds are dipped into hot water, which releases more whey, and then the cheese is stretched and kneaded. This process is used not only for mozzarella, but also for provolone and Oaxaca cheeses, too. "You burn your fin-gers if you do it by hand," says Vito Girardi, third-generation Italian cheesemaker and owner of Gioia Cheese Company. Usually, how-ever, this process of kneading the cheese is done by machine to pre-vent the burning of hands.

After the wheels, balls, or blocks are removed from the molds, the process of aging, or *affinage,* begins. Fresh cheeses like

© PAOLO VESCIA

At Harley Farms, chèvre rounds are formed by hand. Dee calls the hands of her cheesemakers her "secret ingredient."

chèvre and mozzarella are ready for sale and do not really require any aging at all.

But every other cheese—from the semisoft to the hard, from the bloomy rinds to the washed rinds, requires aging. This is often where the art of cheesemaking is taken to a new level. Historically, in France, many times this process was taken on by the *affineur,* who would tend to the care of the cheeses after the cheesemaker made them. Here, however, cheesemakers do it themselves. During the process of *affinage,* sometimes cheeses are washed, sprayed, waxed, or salted to get a different effect.

Bloomy rind cheeses, also known as soft ripened, are aged for two months or less. The ripening happens from just under the white rind and makes its way toward the center of the cheese. You can always tell if the rind was commodity created or handcrafted just by looking at it, says Jim Boyce, owner of Marin French Cheese Company. Perfectly uniform rinds mean that the cheese was created by machine—it was sprayed with culture on the outside so that it looks perfect; if it was handcrafted, the cultures were mixed into it during the process, and it doesn't always look perfect. Besides Brie and Camembert, California has several American original cheeses that have such rinds, like Cowgirl Creamery's Mt. Tam or Cypress Grove's Humboldt Fog.

An ash coating is applied by hand to rounds of Humboldt Fog.

Semisoft cheeses are also aged for a month or two, and they often have irregular holes or eyes in them because they're not pressed as hard as firm or hard cheeses are. Teleme is one great semisoft cheese that is created in California. Havarti is another semisoft variety.

Hard or firm cheeses can be aged from 60 days to several years. Bandage-wrapped cheddar, like the Fiscalini cheese that beat the English cheeses in the World Cheese Awards, is

CYPRESS GROVE CHÈVRE

one such hard cheese. Dry Jack is another popular hard cheese made in California. Many hard cheeses are made from raw or unpasteurized milk. The longer a cheese ages, the more depth of flavor it will develop, and cheeses taste differently at different ages in the process. But it's not just the aged cheeses that taste differently—even a semisoft or bloomy rind cheese will taste a bit differently in the weeks or short months that it ages. But fresh cheeses are never meant to be aged—either in a warehouse or your refrigerator—and they should be consumed within a day or two of purchase.

After cheeses are aged to the point cheesemakers consider them to be at their best, they are packaged, marketed, and sold. Some sell them directly to the consumers through phone or Internet sales or at farmers' markets. Others use distributors who sell them to restaurants and stores. This is the last step in the cheesemaking process, and often, cheesemakers worry about their cheeses when they leave their hands. "When you serve good cheese, there have to be all the right connections from the land to the final person who actually serves the cheese to you," says Soyoung Scanlan, of Andante Dairy. "Sometimes, somebody makes a mistake between the time I made the cheese and when they finally get to eat it. I am concerned about that."

TOP: *Cheese is salted at Harley Farms.* BOTTOM: *Cheese is packed by hand at Marin French Cheese Company.*

CHAPTER 3

The Cheesemakers of
NORTHERN
CALIFORNIA

Ig Vella shows off a wheel of his award-winning Dry Jack.

VELLA CHEESE COMPANY

315 Second Street East
Sonoma, CA 95476
800-848-0505
www.vellacheese.com
COW'S MILK CHEESES

*I*gnazio "Ig" Vella was an artisan cheesemaker before there was such a profession. Vella doesn't have any formal training in the ways of dairy—he majored in history at the University of Santa Clara—but he not only knows his cheese, he knows more than most cheesemakers in the country, if not the world.

Ig, who has more than seven decades of cheesemaking experience, learned first from his father, Tom, who started the Vella Cheese Company in downtown Sonoma in an aged stone building that was originally a brewery—the building was built in 1904. "Whatever I learned, I learned between the vats [of cheese]," Ig says.

Ig's cheese schooling started in November 1931 when his father founded Vella Cheese. "I was three and a half years old," Ig says. His father, who was originally from Italy, had been working at Sonoma Mission Creamery since the early 1920s. He decided to start his own business after a group of local dairymen approached him and promised to supply him with the quality bulk milk he'd need to make cheese.

Tom Vella initially specialized in Monterey Jack cheese, and when demand from Italian immigrants for a good grating cheese arose, he also started making Dry Jack. "Only two of us still make this cheese in the world," Ig says. During World War II, his plant worked around the clock to help supply troops, and Vella Cheese Company was one of the 60 West Coast plants that Kraft purchased cheese from.

Ig remembers when the milk arrived at the factory in cans. He also remembers meeting J. L. Kraft for the first time when he was in the sixth grade. "I got to go to lunch at Fisherman's Wharf in San Francisco," Ig recalls. "He'd take me out of school, and that's how I got to know J. L. Kraft." At the meeting, Kraft gave him a bit of advice.

"He said 'Son, in order to have a good business and sustainability, everybody has to make a profit, and then it's worthwhile to

One of Ig's cheesemakers shows off some of his great cheese.

stay in business. You need to have a good product at a good price,'" Ig says. "Everybody has got to make a living and put some profit aside. I think we haven't gotten away from this. It's the sharp elbow technique."

Ig formally took over the business from his father in 1981, and today he continues to run it. Ig doesn't make cheese all by himself anymore—he has noted cheesemaker Charles Malkassian in charge of production—but he and his small staff continue to make cheese the way his father did—by hand, in small quantities. He also receives the same, high quality of milk his father did, and for the last 20 years the milk has come from the same dairy, from George F. Mertens Sr.'s cows in nearby Schellville.

Over the years Ig has introduced other cheeses to the company's lineup, including Mezzo Secco, which is halfway between a dry and a regular Jack. Mezzo Secco was first developed in the 1930s, back when people used iceboxes instead of refrigerators; cheese lovers wanted a Jack that wasn't as dry as Dry Jack but wasn't as perishable as regular Jack during the hot California summers. During his years of cheesemaking he revived some artisan cheeses that had fallen out of fashion: Toma, a soft cheese from the Piedmont area of Italy (Vella is the only U.S. cheesemaker to craft this), and Romanello, which is like Romano except it is made with cow's milk instead of sheep's milk. Vella also was the first California cheesemaker to make a real Colby cheese. "I always feel you have to have a market for it, and then, can you make it?" Ig says. "The question then is how much will it cost you to produce it, the economic balance."

As well as being the first California cheesemaker to make Colby, Ig also makes a great cheddar. His cheeses have won dozens of awards over the years, including taking top honors at many competitions. "Our cheeses have done very well," Ig says, modestly.

A Marin French Cheese Company cheesemaker loads a tray of freshly made Brie in the aging room in the early 1900s.

MARIN FRENCH CHEESE CO.

7500 Red Hill Road
Petaluma, CA 94952
800-292-6001
www.marinfrenchcheese.com
COW'S MILK AND GOAT'S MILK
SOFT-RIPENED CHEESES

Almost 150 years old, Marin French Cheese Co. is the oldest continually operating cheese factory in the entire United States. Founded in 1865—the same year the Civil War ended and just 15 years after California became the 31st state in the union—Marin French boasts a long, artisanal history, and it keeps reinventing itself and pushing the culinary boundaries of its cheeses.

Its history started with Jefferson A. Thompson, who founded the company as Thompson Bros. Cheese Co. on the same 700-acre site where it operates today. Thompson was a visionary, and he thought there might be a market for the up-and-coming port town of Yerba Buena (which is now San Francisco). When the California gold rush went bust, wannabe miners headed to the port town for dock work, which created a shortage of eggs—pickled eggs were the preferred munchie of choice in Yerba Buena's saloons. And so Thompson created a fresh cheese, Breakfast Cheese, which he shipped to the town to substitute for the desired eggs. "It was meant to be eaten with beer," says Marin French owner Jim Boyce. "It was to provide nourishment for dockworkers."

Because Petaluma shipped food, supplies, and tan oak bark to Yerba Buena via the

Visitors to Marin French often picnic outside its headquarters.

Petaluma River, Thompson was able to get more cheese to this new marketplace than many other cheesemakers. The company continued to evolve, and in the early 1900s it was organized as the Marin French Cheese Co., one of California's first small corporations. The company branched out into other cheese varieties including Neufchâtel and cream cheese, but more importantly, it began making soft-ripened European varieties such as Camembert and Schloss. "We are always pushing the envelope of what the market is looking for," Jim says.

Another evolvement occurred in 1930, during the Great Depression. To support neighboring herds and to concentrate on cheesemaking, the company discontinued milking its own herd and purchased milk from neighbors. To this day, the milk comes from neighboring, rBST-free (recombinant bovine somatotropin-free) herds.

And the cheese is made in the same, handcrafted tradition that Thompson started. Although computers and automation play a role in many aspects of the business, each of the more than 40 different cheese varieties are all made by hand in small batches. "It's really a testament to what this factory is about," Jim says. "It's the milk source and the traditional methods that make our cheeses special. Cheeses that are manipulated by machinery are not the same. We've seen World Wars, the Depression, and more. We make cheese. We handcraft it. We listen to the market, determine the direction it's going."

Marin French is determined to make great cheese, Jim says. And starting in the 1980s it finally began getting recognition, first modestly taking third place in categories at the American Cheese Society competition. But in 2005 it took on international cheeses, and at the World Cheese Awards in London, its triple crème Brie, goat's milk blue Brie, and Yellow Buck Chèvre Camembert took gold awards, with the Yellow Buck winning the trophy for best American cheese. Its triple crème Brie award, however, garnered the most international press, as it was the first time an American Brie beat the French. "When we beat France, it was written up in France, but it was hard to get a write-up in the United States," Jim says.

Then in 2007 another triple crème Brie, Marin French Gold, beat the French the same year that Fiscalini Cheese's traditional bandaged cheddar beat the English, and thus, like the Judgment of Paris showed the world how good California wines are, the Judgment of London showed the world how good California cheese is.

Marin French's Brie has won worldwide accolades and awards.

Marin French's goat's milk cheeses start with local herds of contented goats.

27

MARIN FRENCH CHEESE CO.

Local herds of Jersey cows provide milk to Marin French Cheese Company.

Today, Marin French ships its cheese not only across California, but some of its cheeses have traveled to Central America, Japan, and South Korea. "It will be a while before it's accepted in England and France," Jim says.

Though Jim enjoys eating his cheese in a variety of ways, he especially recommends serving his triple crème cheeses with champagne. "Almost freeze the triple crème, then shave a little bit of it off," Jim advises. "Take one sip of champagne with that little snowflake of triple crème . . . it's wonderful."

ACHADINHA CHEESE COMPANY

750 Chileno Valley Road

Petaluma, CA 94952

707-763-1025

www.achadinha.com

FARMSTEAD AGED GOAT'S MILK CHEESES

The dairy business runs in Donna and Jim Pacheco's blood. Jim's family's farm started in 1953 in Bodega Bay, and the dairy was moved to a 358-acre site in Petaluma in 1969. A third-generation dairyman, Jim had grown up with cows, and he and Donna continued the family tradition with their four children, William, 16; Daniel, 11; Elizabeth, 9; and David, 7.

But in the 1990s, when many cow dairies had to expand in order to survive, Donna and Jim looked at another option: goat dairying. "There was a great demand for goat's milk," Donna says. Because goats seemed to offer better opportunities for selling their milk, they sold the cows and bought goats in 1997. "It was hard for my husband," Donna says.

They had to learn an entirely new way of running a dairy, and they had to learn about goats, which are quite different from cows. "There was a lot of research we had to do," Donna says. "When we started, we had to ask a lot of questions."

Not only did they end up changing their dairy operations, but they also added a farm-stead cheese component to their operations, calling it Achadinha (pronounced Osh-a-deen-a), after the region in Portugal that Jim's family is from. "We made a lot of really bad cheeses in the process of learning," Donna says. "It's just part of experimenting and doing what you can."

But luckily for cheese lovers everywhere, they kept at it. In 2002 their aged Capricious cheese took top honors at the American Cheese Society, winning Best in Show. That was less than five years after they transitioned into goat dairying.

Capricious is a delicious cheese that is aged for up to 10 months and rubbed with olive oil. Besides Capricious, they also make Broncha, which is aged up to 6 months, and fresh, salt-brined feta that Donna crafts by hand. They also make a delicious goat summer sausage, too.

Because their herd of 1,200 goats is allowed to roam and browse on the extensive pasturelands of their farm, their milk is quite sought after. In fact, Donna and Jim sell their milk to many other artisan dairy operators, including Laloo's, Redwood Hill, Marin French, and Spring Hill Jersey. "We only use a little bit of milk for our cheese," Donna says.

This year they're moving all of their cheesemaking operations on-site to their farm, and they hope to be able to invite visitors to their farm by 2009. "Agritourism is so important," Donna says. "It's important for people to understand where their food is coming from. It's a great experience, especially for city kids."

ANDANTE DAIRY

5450 Red Hill Road

Petaluma, CA 94952

707-769-1379

www.andantedairy.com

COW'S MILK AND GOAT'S MILK BLOOMY RIND CHEESES

A trip to Europe and feasting on wonderful cheese there led Soyoung Scanlan into her life's passion. "From these simple ingredients—milk, culture, and salt—the variety of final tastes I could experience was actually amazing," Soyoung says. "I became very interested. I was trying to do something related to food, and something I could do with my hands."

Soyoung, who had an academic background in food engineering and biochemistry, returned from that trip with her husband determined to make cheese. To begin, she enrolled in a dairy science Ph.D. course at Cal Poly, and in 2000 she first began making cheese with the help of Barbara Backus at Goat's Leap. "I started with cow's milk because that was mostly available, and I'd only use Jersey milk," Soyoung says.

Later she began using goat's milk, and sometimes she combines both goat's milk and cow's milk into singular cheeses. "The different milks complement each other," Soyoung says. "In the summer here, cow's milk is not very good because of the weather, the flavor is too dry, but goats tend to like the drier weather. Working with both milks, I can change the amounts of cheese I make by blending, and I can actually adjust to the quality changes in the milk."

Each of the cheeses she creates is very personal to her, and the names of both her company and her cheeses come from her great love of music. An accomplished pianist, she plays the piano every day, and she named her company from that passion. "It's easier to find a name, some kind of clue, from what you love the most, and classical music has been there for me from the day I was born," she says. "It didn't make any sense to my husband. He said 'Music and cheese? Isn't that weird?' But it's a very personal thing."

Music, she says, is something that she connects to everything in life. "When I see some beautiful scenery, a certain theme or symphony comes to mind," Soyoung says. "Every cheese has a very personal meaning for me. If somebody loves music, and many of my customers do, we talk about music. It's just what I love."

All of her cheeses are soft ripened, with beautiful bloomy rinds, and she follows traditional French ways of making cheese. "It has to be cream and softness and a balance of flavor, and when it's aged, the intensity of flavor builds," she says. "Cheese is not just a simple food. To make good cheese, you have to have a good milk, and to have a good milk you have to have healthy animals. When you have a good cheese, there are these connections to the land, and it's an accumulation of work. To have a cheese with really good flavor, it's more like a symphony, with each person playing his part."

Slowly, Soyoung is growing her company, and her output increases by about 20 percent a year. But her production is exceeded by the demand for her cheeses, and she has a long waiting list of customers. "Yes, my business is getting bigger, but my existing customers are taking more cheese," she says.

Soyoung doesn't want to grow her business too big. She likes working alone, and she likes to be able to control the quality of her cheeses, from start to finish. "I always think about the definition of what being truly artisanal means, and I want to stay very focused, to be myself," she says. "I love that intimate kind of atmosphere."

Because she's not really taking too many new customers, the best way for caseophiles to meet her is to go to the Ferry Plaza Farmers Market in San Francisco. She's there every weekend, and she likes meeting people who appreciate her cheese. "I have very beautiful customers," she says.

BELFIORE CHEESE COMPANY

2031-A 2nd Street
Berkeley, CA 94710
510-540-5500
1-800-610-FARM
www.belfiorecheese.com
COW'S MILK MOZZARELLA, FETA, RICOTTA

*S*andwiched between some railroad tracks and a humane society animal shelter in Berkeley is one of the most urban, artisan cheese plants in California, if not the entire country. Belfiore Cheese Company is a small, family-run operation, but they make some really good cheese.

The company was started by an Italian family in 1987, but Farr Hariri took over the company in 1990. Farr, who initially came to California from Iran for graduate school, got involved in the gourmet foods industry in 1981 when he founded Kaspian Sea Gourmet, which specialized in importing caviars. Hariri noticed a growing interest in cheese in the 1980s, and he saw a need for domestically produced feta cheese. "There was very little feta in the domestic market," Farr says.

He found a small cheese company, and he decided it would be there that he would learn the ins and the outs of the cheesemaking business. "I was looking for another opportunity, and it was small enough to get started," Farr says.

Farr moved the company's operations to a small building in Berkeley that had originally been a milk bottling plant. "We had to redo everything, but it was the main structure that was important."

Initially, Farr kept to the company's original offerings of fresh mozzarella varieties, but he experimented with different feta recipes that first year, and then in 1991 he began producing it, and it took off. "I'm a staunch believer that in order to be good at something, you have to start from the ground up," Farr says. "We took our time, both in terms of market and product expansions. We only grew a few percentage points every year. We're still really small, but obviously we're a lot larger than when we started."

Though production has increased over the years since Hariri began, the company remains small and family run. Farr wears a variety of hats himself, and his wife, Mojgan, helps out. The operations are run by only six people. "We only buy our milk from handlers we know, and we certify that all of our milk is rBST-free," Farr says.

Today, the company makes not only regular mozzarella and feta, but it also makes smoked mozzarella, farmer's cheese, and most recently added paneer, a fresh Indian cheese, to its lineup. Farr's cheeses have won several awards from the American Cheese Society and World Championship Cheese Competition, but perhaps his company's most notable cheese is its smoked mozzarella.

Most smoked cheeses are not really smoked—they're infused with liquid smoke. Belfiore's smoked cheese is actually smoked in a real smoker, with apple chips, elder wood, and cherry wood chips. "I usually detect bitterness, an aftertaste, in cheeses made with liquid smoke," Farr says. "Elder wood gives us the aroma, cherry gives us a hint of flavor, and apple gives our cheese its color. The result is a very milky cheese with a sweetness."

BELLWETHER FARMS

9999 Valley Ford Road
Petaluma, CA 94952
888-527-8606
www.bellwetherfarms.com
SHEEP'S MILK CHEESE AND YOGURT, COW'S MILK CHEESE, AND CRÈME FRAÎCHE

When Cindy Callahan, a former attorney, and her late husband, Ed, a physician, purchased their farmland in Petaluma in 1986, it was just going to be an escape from city life. They got into sheep almost accidentally, as Cindy acquired the sheep to keep the pasture grasses on their 34 acres from getting out of control. That led them into the cheese business.

Cindy, Ed, and their son, Liam, opened their creamery in 1990, and it was one of the first sheep dairies in the country. Their first cheeses were made from fresh milk, but in order to make the great, aged sort of cheeses that they were aiming for, they realized they needed a little more training, so Cindy and Liam headed out to the Tuscany and Umbria regions of Italy in 1992. "My mother and I spent a month in Italy," Liam says.

Then in 1994 Liam returned again to continue in his journey as a cheesemaker. That same year Liam also added some cow's milk cheeses to expand their lineup and offer cheeses year-round, using the milk from a neighbor's herd of Jersey cows. "It's been a learning curve," he says. "Dealing with logistics, point of sale, etc. . . . there's a lot more to it than just having a great, great cheese."

Liam's cheeses have won numerous awards and recognition from top food publications like *Gourmet*. In 2006, Liam's San Andreas American original sheep's milk cheese won a gold medal in the semihard sheep's milk cheese category at the World Cheese Awards in London. In the same competition, his Jersey milk Carmody took a bronze medal in the semihard, unpressed cow's milk category. As a result of their fine quality, his cheeses are used by top chefs throughout the country. Over the years, Liam has added and changed cheeses in his lineup, and this year he began making sheep's milk yogurt. "The best cheese in the world comes from sheep's milk," Liam says.

So it's no surprise that it also makes great yogurt. The yogurt is richer than cow's milk yogurts and has received rave reviews from yogurt lovers. "It's been really eye opening," Liam says. "People can't believe how good it is. And we've learned that there's a passionate group of yogurt lovers out there."

While Liam continues with his innovations in cheese and dairy products, Cindy continues to tend to her herd of 200 sheep, including 150 ewes for milking. Her East Friesian flock is pastured on rolling hills just a few miles from the Pacific Ocean, and no herbicides or artificial fertilizers are ever used on the land. The lambs—East Friesians are known for having one to three and sometimes as many as five lambs each year—are fed by their mothers for 45 days, and after that, the ewes are milked for about eight months. Since the Callahans feel strongly about doing things naturally, no artificial hormones are ever used to increase or prolong milk production. "My mother is in charge of the sheep," Liam says. "She's seventy-three years old and still going strong."

COWGIRL CREAMERY

80 Fourth Street
Point Reyes Station, CA 94956
415-663-9335
www.cowgirlcreamery.com
ORGANIC COW'S MILK CHEESES

Inside the cheese store at Cowgirl Creamery.

With a name like Cowgirl Creamery, you know you're a million miles from ordinary. Headquartered in a renovated old hay barn in Point Reyes Station, this little organic creamery has made a big splash in the cheese world.

It started out first as a culinary philosophy, a way of life if you will, for the original cowgirls, Sue Conley and Peggy Smith. Sue and Peggy are gourmet chefs who met at the University of Tennessee and after graduation moved out to California. Peggy was a chef/kitchen coordinator at Chez Panisse for 17 years, and Sue owned Bette's Oceanview Diner. "Sue and I both come from cooking backgrounds," Peggy says. "We both started out with really good basic ingredients and promotion of really good land management."

In 1994 they came together with the idea of promoting all of the wonderful family-owned dairy farms in Marin and Sonoma counties to showcase the agricultural heritage of the region, and that's how they opened Tomales Bay Foods. In 1997 they took their marketing venture a step further and jumped into a business they had contemplated all along: cheesemaking.

Using only the rich organic milk from Straus Family Creamery, the two began by making fresh cheeses—*fromage blanc,* clabbered (cream added) cottage cheese, and the like, and that's when they changed their name to Cowgirl Creamery. "We wanted to promote the organic milk the dairy worked so hard to produce," Peggy says.

Though Cowgirl still makes fresh cheeses, they are more known for their amazing aged, bloomy rind cheeses. The first one they made was Mt. Tam, named for Mount Tamalpais, which can be seen north of San Francisco Bay. This decadent triple crème wows just about everyone who tries it, and it really showcases the richness of the milk.

But perhaps even more well known is their Red Hawk, which was actually a mistake. A batch of Mt. Tam became contaminated with a locally found bacterium, turning the ivory cheese a reddish hue. This naturally occurring mistake was a wonder, and in 2003, it took Best in Show honors at the American Cheese Society competition. Besides Red Hawk and Mt.

Cowgirl Creamery offers a gorgeous selection of artisan cheeses from around the world in their lovely store.

Tam, they also make two seasonal bloomy rinds: Pierce Point, a fall and winter cheese that is washed in muscato wine and herbs; and St. Pat, which is wrapped with stinging nettles (the nettles are frozen first and thus made stingless).

Red Hawk isn't their only award-winning cheese—all of their fresh cheeses have won first-place prizes in their categories at the American Cheese Society annual competitions from 1997 until 2006, and in fact, every one of their cheeses has won competitions. Mt. Tam and

Pierce Point have won first place in the American Cheese Society, too. In 2006 they were also inducted by the James Beard Foundation into the Who's Who in American Food. "The brand is bigger than we are," Peggy says.

Their Point Reyes Station creamery, which has a gorgeous viewing window and offers tours every Friday, not only highlights their cheeses, but it also features artisanal cheeses from around the state, and indeed, around the globe. "Our goal is to promote all small producers, not just Cowgirl," Peggy explains. Their store boasts a gourmet deli and shop, to boot.

Cowgirl also operates a retail store in the Ferry Building in San Francisco, and another shop across the country, in Washington, D.C. Still, all their cheese is manufactured in small batches and by hand. Last year they expanded to have another cheesemaking facility in the Foundry Wharf Business Park, a few miles down the road in Petaluma. The new plant will allow them greater freedom to experiment in crafting different cheeses. However, they still make Red Hawk and their delicious, clabbered cottage cheese at their original facility, and you can still tour their original plant. "Tours demystify the process, and a lot of people don't even understand milk," Peggy says. "A lot of cheesemaking has to do with the milk you start with, your desire to make great cheese, and your closeness to market. We're lucky in that we have a lot of farmers' markets near us."

CYPRESS GROVE CHÈVRE

1330 Q Street
Arcata, CA 95521
707-825-1100
www.cypressgrovechevre.com
FRESH, BLOOMY RIND AND AGED
GOAT'S MILK CHEESE

CYPRESS GROVE CHÈVRE

Cypress Grove cheese started with the goats.

*M*ary Keehn never intended to become a pioneer for goat's milk or goat's milk cheeses. She simply was a mother who wanted good quality milk for her daughters. "I was the 4-H mom for a dairy goat project, and I got involved in showing goats," Mary says. "They did really well, and we had four national champions for Alpine goats, and pretty soon, you've got fifty goats."

And with that many goats Mary had a surplus of milk, so she started making cheese in her kitchen, and it turned out that not only did Mary have the right touch for breeding goats, she also had a knack for making cheese. In 1983 she launched her cheese company. "We started with ten thousand dollars, and I had four kids so I had to make it work," Mary says. "When I first started, my parents tried really hard to talk me out of it."

Her four daughters—Mallory, Holly, Sarah, and Jolene—and their friends all pitched in, helping wrap cheese, put labels on it, and package it for sale. Because they lived in rural Humboldt County, in an area closer to Oregon than most major cities, Mary knew that her little company couldn't survive by selling her goat's milk chèvre just in the area. "Early on, we decided to work with distributors," Mary says.

Slowly her cheeses began to develop a following, and in the late 1980s Mary and her friend Judy Schad, of Capriole Goat Cheese in Indiana, makers of Wabash Cannonball cheese, headed to France to learn the intricacies of making aged goat's milk cheeses. They visited noted cheesemaker and gourmet Chantal Plasse, who arranged tours for them throughout France. "We both came back and decided to do those kinds of cheeses," Mary says. "Judy started with the Wabash Cannonball, and I came up with Humboldt Fog."

Humboldt Fog is one of those truly beautiful cheeses. A bloomy rind cheese, it is coated with ash on the outside, with a delicate line of ash in the middle. "It was the right time for those cheeses, as people were traveling more," Mary says. Humboldt Fog not only has won awards, but its memorable name sticks in people's minds.

Around the same time that Mary created Humboldt Fog, she also created a cheese called Sempervirens, taking its name from the scientific name for Northern California's giant redwoods. That name confused people, and Mary ultimately ended up discontinuing its production. "I learned two things from that time," Mary says.

Mary shows one of her lovely cheeses.

Just steps away from where this company picture was taken is where employees play soccer every day during their lunch break.

CYPRESS GROVE CHÈVRE

CYPRESS GROVE CHÈVRE

Vegetable ash is added by hand to wheels of Humboldt Fog cheese.

Goats are inquisitive animals, and they're willing to stop eating to greet visitors.

"Copies of French cheeses were not as accepted as original cheeses. Make your own cheese, and then give it a name that people can pronounce. It was a good cheese, but it was a poor name."

Since then Mary's cheeses have had more accessible names—Fog Lights, Purple Haze, and Truffle Tremor—to name but a few. To augment her line of fresh and bloomy rind cheeses, Mary has worked with cheesemakers in Holland to come up with some aged cheeses, Midnight Moon and Lamb Chopper (a sheep's milk cheese). Since she didn't have room for building another aging room, she looked to other innovative cheesemakers with whom she could partner. "We couldn't make another cheese," Mary says. "In Holland, the land is really scarce so their husbandry is really phenomenal. Now, we get to go to Holland every year."

Mary and her talented team still come up with new cheeses, but "there has to be a reason for a new cheese," Mary says. They also work hard at coming up with other innovations for their cheeses. They now have their own special wrapping paper for their cheese, and the cardboard containers that the cheeses are shipped in are like small, contained aging rooms, which makes it easier for stores and distributors. "We're always looking for ways to improve," Mary says.

About 14 years ago Mary sold off her goats, and she now purchases milk from family farms in Humboldt County. All of the goats are still pasture grazed, and Cypress Grove works closely with the dairies to ensure the quality of the milk is exactly what they want.

Mary credits Cypress Grove's longevity—it just celebrated 25 years—to her employees, many of whom can be found on their lunch break every day playing soccer in the parking lot. And if you walk through her little factory, you'll hear many of them singing, laughing, and generally enjoying their jobs. "The culture's not just in the cheese," Mary says. "That's the key—to enjoy what you do because then it allows you to do a good job. This is my calling."

DÉLICE DE LA VALLÉE/
THE EPICUREAN CONNECTION

P.O. Box 1916

Sonoma, CA 95476

707-935-7960

sheana@vom.com

www.sheanadavis.com

TRIPLE CRÈME COW'S MILK AND GOAT'S MILK CHEESE

Sheana Davis is an enthusiastic champion of California artisan foods. Chef, caterer, and culinary educator, Sheana is passionate about locally cultivated foods, especially those made by artisan cheesemakers, winemakers, and brewmasters.

Sheana shares her ardor for these great foods at the many events she hosts, arranges, or attends as a guest speaker, and since 1992 when she formed her company, The Epicurean Connection, she's promoted more than a dozen creameries, wineries, and craft breweries and their products. "For me, the inspiration is the families and the faces behind the cheeses," Sheana says. "Each farm and family is in the cheese business because they have the passion for the products they produce and it's always reflected in the taste of the amazing cheeses they have created."

But in the decades that she's been advocating the foods of Sonoma County, including the annual hosting of the Sonoma Valley Cheese Conference, something was missing. "I felt like I was always promoting someone else's cheese," says Sheana. "I was making blends of cheese in my catering company for years, and friends encouraged me to make my own cheese."

With their support and encouragement, Sheana began experimenting in her kitchen in 2005. Her friend Jim Yonkus helped her refine her cheese, and after numerous batches and taste testings, Sheana came up with a creamy, delicious cheese. "It was inspired by my friend Jim," Sheana says. "He really encouraged me to evolve and create a new cheese."

But Sheana didn't know quite what to call her new cheese. Knowing her passion for Sonoma Valley's bounty, her friend Kathy Hargitt suggested that she call it "Délice de La Vallée." The name, which means "a delicacy of the valley," resonated with Sheana, who happens to be a fourth-generation Sonoma Valley native, and the cheese reflects the bounty of the valley. "It's just exciting to see Sheana debut this cheese," says Kathy. "She does an incredible amount of charity work, and she's known by everyone here."

Délice de La Vallée just made its debut last spring, making it one of the newest artisan cheeses created in California, and it is one of only a handful of mixed milk cheeses crafted in the state, as it is half goat's milk and half cow's milk. A triple crème cheese, it has both savory and sweet uses, and often at catering events Sheana serves the cheese with an array of accompaniments, from sun-dried tomatoes to golden raspberries, rose petal jelly to balsamic vinegar and honey reductions.

"I like to point out that it is similar to chèvre and *fromage blanc*, but it's richer and creamier," Sheana says. "There's not another fresh, cow-goat cheese made. It has the flavor of goat, but the consistency of *fromage blanc*."

Délice de La Vallée made its entrance to the national market at a culinary event in New Orleans, where it earned raves. One chef who tasted Sheana's Délice told her "Oh, my gosh, we have to get it here in New Orleans."

It also remains a favorite among Sheana's friends and fans closer to home. "I eat it for breakfast on toast with a boiled egg," says Kathy.

Sheana is more than satisfied with her new creation. "I love the name; Délice de la Vallée, delicacy of the valley. My valley, my Sonoma," Sheana says.

GOAT'S LEAP CHEESE

3321 St. Helena Highway

St. Helena, CA 94574

707-963-2337

www.goatsleap.com

FRESH CHÈVRE, BLOOMY RIND, AND AGED GOAT'S MILK CHEESES

Barbara and Rex Backus moved up to Napa Valley in 1972 to escape urban living in Los Angeles, and they bought some land north of St. Helena. "We purchased sixty-four acres of rock and dirt, which is not a farm," says Barbara.

They discovered that the rough terrain was good for goats, and since they loved animals, they decided to get a couple of Angora goats for fiber and La Mancha goats for milk. "The dairy goats won out," Barbara says. In the mid-1980s they decided to build a dairy, and they sold milk to a cheesemaker. Barbara started making cheese for home consumption, and then they decided to build a farmstead creamery. "The bigger problem was acquiring small-scale equipment, which was not available in the late '80s," Barbara says. "You just had to keep your ear to the ground and find out what junkyard had what you needed and hope that you could acquire it."

In 1992 Barbara and Rex were able to get their hands on the right equipment, which they had to fix up so it would exactly suit their needs. "What makes our cheese unique is that it is a single breed in a single herd that provides the milk and one cheesemaker who makes the cheese," Barbara says. "That tends to individualize any cheese automatically."

Their herd currently numbers 12, and it ranges from 12 to 24, but they don't like it to get too large. "I do the milking and the cheesemaking, and Rex does everything else," Barbara says. "We don't really want to spend eight to ten hours a day out there, as that's what burns people out. I am aware of what my capabilities are, and they're really limited."

Her limited production allows her to make the highest quality cheeses she can, so her cheeses are mostly available in Napa and Sonoma counties and sometimes as far as San Francisco, but not really any farther. Barbara crafts everything from a fresh chèvre to an aged Carmela, and she also crafts some cheeses that are wrapped in fig leaves and ash, too.

Her cheeses get their unique flavors not only due to her handcrafting, but also to the browsing the goats enjoy on their terrain. Besides hay and grain, they get to browse on the hillside, snacking on whatever untouched flora tastes best to them. Barbara makes cheese with their milk only 10 months out of the year, letting her goats rest for 2 months.

What she loves best about the cheesemaking is the goats. "What's not to enjoy?" Barbara says. "They are all individuals, and I enjoy the uniqueness of each goat."

© PAOLO VESCIA

ABOVE: *A cheesemaker shows off gorgeous rounds of chèvre.* RIGHT: *A goat grazes on farm pasture just outside the creamery.*

HARLEY FARMS GOAT DAIRY

205 North Street

Pescadero, CA 94060

650-879-0480

www.harleyfarms.com

GOAT'S MILK CHEESES—FRESH CHÈVRE, RICOTTA, TORTES, FETA

Out of the package, most fresh chèvres look pretty much the same—nicely molded patties, logs, or containers of chalk-white goodness. But Dee Harley's chèvre rounds are readily identifiable, with or without any packaging. Each is molded, by hand, with edible flowers. Blue bachelor buttons, red geraniums, and violet Johnny-jump-ups, all grown in a gorgeous little garden just behind her farm store.

Dee's floral-accented creations are simply the prettiest chèvre around, and her signature style was born of necessity. When she started, she couldn't afford to hire a graphic designer to come up with a logo so she innovatively decided to use edible flowers. "It has become our trademark," Dee says.

Though Dee's herd and farm has grown in the 15 years she's been milking goats, each lovely disk is still molded by hand, and she calls her talented assistants' hands a "secret ingredient" in

© PAOLO VESCIA

her cheeses. "Everything is very gentle here," Dee says. "We're not in a rush."

Dee's organically cultivated (but not certified) 11 acres were originally part of a small cow dairy farm owned by a Portuguese family a century ago. When Dee and her husband purchased the farm it had become run down, and they salvaged it, piece by piece, bringing its inherent beauty back to the surface. "We all feel a sense of connection, that the farm is being cared for," says Ryan Andrus, farm manager.

Caring for the farm, the animals, and the people is part and parcel of who Harley is. Born in Yorkshire, England, Dee had dreamed of being a farmer as a young girl, but her yearning for travel and adventure led her eventually to San Mateo County in California. She started out in agriculture by importing tomatoes, but then a local woman offered to sell Dee her goats. She bought three. "Then three became six, and six became twelve," Dee says.

Dee fell in love with goats, and she sold her milk to a cheesemaker. Around the same time she was getting interested in

Goats browse on pastures that are tinged with the salt of the nearby ocean.

Visitors to Harley Farms are encouraged to interact with the goats.

© PAOLO VESCIA

ABOVE: *Flowers are picked fresh just before they are added to the chèvre.* RIGHT: *All the herbs and flowers are carefully molded to the cheese by hand.*

cheesemaking, the cheesemaker who purchased her milk was interested in leaving. "She was ready to go, and I was ready to get into the business," Dee says.

Dee started small, with simple chèvres that she decorated with edible flowers grown on the farm, but her line has since grown to encompass various nuts, fruits, and herbs, and she now makes feta, ricotta, and *fromage blanc.* She's won numerous awards and was named Farmer of the Year in San Mateo County in 2008.

The farm itself is moving into the realm of biodynamics, with crop rotations and innovative farming techniques, such as using a moveable hutch of chickens down the field to fertilize, break down goat waste, and keep pests down. The goats are rotationally grazed among the ocean-touched pastures, and the chickens move with them to help nature along. Besides the 220 goats, the farm has 5 sheep, 3 llamas, 2 cows, and 70 chickens. "The llamas are the herd's protectors from coyotes, bobcats, and even the cougar," Ryan says.

© PAOLO VESCIA

The cheesemaking operation is right next to the pastures, and the milk is gently pumped from the milk house and then equally gently pasteurized so that the cheese comes out as delicate tasting as the fresh milk. It is then sold right next door, in a gem of a farmstead shop, which is even painted with goat milk paint. Above the shop is an elegant yet rustic gathering space, where local chefs sometimes host dinners. Every Fourth of July the farm also hosts a picnic.

Weekdays, schoolchildren tour the farm, but on weekends, that's when city folk come down from San Francisco to experience agricultural life and take a tour. "They're all searching for a piece of this," Dee says. "They want to feel good, and when they buy a piece of cheese, they can take the feeling with them."

Visitors can take in the Pacific Ocean, too, which is just a stone's throw from the farm, and some people even find its presence in the cheeses themselves. "At the Terre Madre Slow Foods (convivium) in Italy, one of the cheese experts said 'Oh, this cheese is made near the ocean,'" Ryan says.

LAURA CHENEL'S CHÈVRE

4310 Fremont Drive

Sonoma, CA 95476

707-996-4477

www.rians.com

FRESH AND BLOOMY RIND

GOAT'S MILK CHEESES

Laura Chenel's Chèvre is one of the most recognizable goat's milk cheeses in the world.

*S*ay the name "Laura Chenel" and fresh, tangy chèvre immediately springs into the minds of gourmets across the globe. Laura Chenel has been and remains an icon in the world of American artisan cheese, and she was one of the first—if not the first—American cheesemaker to ever produce and sell real chèvre on American soil.

Her story—and that of the entire new food movement in California—is the stuff of legend. In the 1970s Laura lived with a handful of goats on a Sonoma County farm. Captivated by the goats—but not a huge drinker of their milk—Laura tried to turn her beloved animals' milk into cheese. Not very good cheese, as she and others recall.

So, like any adventurous pioneer, she thought outside the box; she journeyed to France, where she worked with goat cheese authority Jean-Claude Le Jaouen to learn the art of making goat's milk cheese. She returned, and in 1979, using French cheese molds, she began making her first cheeses. One of her very first customers was the legendary chef Alice Waters, who fell in love with Laura's soft, yummy cheeses. Thus Chenel introduced the American public to goat's milk cheese, and by the 1980s demand soared. Along the way she worked with Ig Vella to come up with the aged Tomme cheese, and that also met with success.

In 1993 she moved her cheesemaking operations from Santa Rosa to the old Clover Stornetta dairy building in Sonoma. Laura's popularity continued to grow, but in 2006 Chenel realized that she had grown the company as far as she wished, and what she desired was to explore other things in her life. So after a careful vetting process, she sold the company to the notable French cheese company Rians Group, which specializes in goat's milk cheeses and owns other small artisanal cheese operations. Chenel's herd of 500 goats still supply the milk for the cheese that bears her name. "She wanted a company that completely shared her values, and there's been a real continuity here in terms of the operations," says Jacquelyn Buchanan, director of culinary development.

What a lot of people don't realize is that the cheese is still made in the same small batches that Laura and her employees crafted and still use her original recipes. The cheese is not imported, as some people misunderstood when Laura sold her operation; in reality it is as artisan as it always was.

The building itself is nondescript and it's easy to miss, as the large sign outside still declares it CLOVER STORNETTA; a smaller sign says LAURA CHENEL. And if you visit their headquarters, you'll notice Chenel's goats eating the decorative flower beds through the fence. The company remains small; there are only 15 employees hand-ladling the curds into molds.

Marie Lesoudier is the new cheesemaker and general manager for Laura Chenel. She has an extensive background in goat's milk cheese-

LAURA CHENEL'S CHÈVRE

Cheesemaker Marie Lesoudier and culinary director Jacquelyn Buchanan relax outside the creamery in a small garden near the goats.

making, including goat husbandry. "For me, it's like magic to see the milk become cheese," Marie says.

Marie has helped grow the line of cheeses to include such wonderful products as Taupinière, a bloomy rind, slightly aged goat cheese that boasts a delicious outer layer of ash. "Marie will expand our line a bit," Buchanan says. "There's a lot more people making goat cheese now, and that wasn't the case when Laura started. What we are doing is a continuation of Laura's great beginning."

LOLETA CHEESE COMPANY

252 Loleta Drive

Loleta, CA 95551

707-733-5470

www.loletacheesecom

*JERSEY COW'S CHEESE AND HIS-
PANIC/LATINO-STYLE CHEESE*

Loleta Cheese is the main attraction in Loleta, California.

 student's question in Bob Laffranchi's agricultural class at Eureka High School led Laffranchi into an entirely new profession, that of cheesemaking. The student asked him "How is cheese made?" "So I gave him $15 and told him to get a book on cheesemaking," Bob recalls. "He comes back with a hippie cookbook, and we used the steam tables at the stadium to make something similar to a cheddar cheese. I think we used buttermilk as the basis for our culture, and then all the jokes started from my coworkers about the head cheese, the big cheese."

That initial cheese might not have been too tasty, but it led Bob and his wife, Carol, into a new profession. Bob grew up in Ferndale, a fourth-generation resident, and he has dairy on both sides of his family's history. In fact, today some of his Jersey cows still live on the farmstead where his mother grew up. He studied dairy and agriculture at Cal Poly, but he hadn't planned on becoming a cheesemaker until his student asked him that question.

In 1982, after studying cheesemaking in a little more depth, he left teaching and purchased an old cabinet shop in downtown Loleta. Earlier that year, before Bob purchased the building, it had been used as a commissary for a film crew that was shooting *Halloween III* in a factory building across the street. "We remodeled the building and started buying milk," Bob

Bob behind the counter with Amy Reohr, inviting visitors to taste samples of all Loleta's cheeses.

says. "We were knocking on every grocery store's door and learning all the lessons you probably should know before you start."

Bob started with Jack and cheddar, and he had one guiding principle—make great cheese. "If we made great cheese, I knew we'd have customers," Bob says.

The great cheese starts with the milk of their 800 mostly Jersey cows. Jersey cows' milk has higher fat content, making their milk perfect for cheesemaking. "You can take and ruin good milk, but you cannot take bad milk and make good cheese," Bob says.

Bob's Jerseys are grazed on picture-perfect rolling hills for most of the year. "In a typical year, they're out in the pastures from March until November," Bob says. "Our soil, our climate, our feed is unique, and it gives us an ability to produce a great product. A lot of people think northern California is San Francisco, but we're Baja Oregon."

Bob and Carol also welcomed visitors to the plant from the beginning, and tourists who come to look at the gorgeous redwoods often end up at their little factory, relaxing in the garden that Carol designed. "We have about 35,000 people who have come to visit us, and they are the most cherished gift," Bob says. "The garden is to slow the world down because it's going too fast."

"My favorite part is creating a place where people can come to visit and enjoy," Carol says.

Bob's initial 2 cheeses have evolved into a line of 35 different cheeses, including many flavored cheeses, as well as fontina, Havarti, and *queso fresco*. When he started they made 2,000 pounds of cheese a week, now they make 40,000 pounds a week. They also ended up taking over some dairies to ensure quality. "We took dairies over that needed some TLC," Bob says.

In 1995 they started making organic cheese when Albert Straus had some excess milk, and in 2006 they converted one of their own farms to organic. "We have never liked using bovine growth hormones," Bob says. "It's like somebody doing a great job for you, and you demand even more from them."

Bob started making *queso fresco* when a customer asked if he could make it because that grocery's current supplier didn't have the quality he was looking for. Because Jersey milk has more carotene in it, it has a yellow tinge, and *queso fresco* must be white. "In the Hispanic market, yellow is bad for a cheese," Bob says. "Even though the cheese made with Jersey milk tastes good, it's not what we use. We actually have a herd of Holstein cows just for making this cheese. We are developing some other make procedures from Mexico for other cheeses. I know there's some market potential there."

Bob also developed a fontina when Wolfgang Puck needed a reliable version for his pizzas. And although Wolfgang Puck is a big customer, Bob

Bob's Jersey calves are friendly to visitors. If you approach them, they will lick your fingers.

treats all of his customers the same. "You need to be diversified if you're little," Bob says. "The other philosophy is we honor all of our retailers the same, even the very small ones. We don't have a minimum order. If you take care of your customers, they'll take care of you."

Eventually, Bob would like to have a little café at his cheese shop and plant to welcome his customers even more. "I'd like to be able to offer some nice coffees, nice drinks, and a limited menu," Bob says.

MID-COAST CHEESE COMPANY (FRANKLIN'S TELEME)

P.O. Box 2456

Los Banos, CA 93635

209-826-6259

www.franklinscheese.com

TELEME

Franklin Peluso is a third-generation cheesemaker. His grandfather, Giovanni Peluso, immigrated to California from Crete, and in 1917 he started a creamery. Giovanni taught his son Frank how to make cheese, and Frank taught Franklin how to make cheese.

Franklin started making cheese in the 1970s for his family's company, Peluso Cheese, and he started making the cheese for which he is famous, Teleme, in 1980. Teleme is one of those American originals—a California original, actually—that is derived from the Italian cheese Stracchino, a semisoft, creamy cheese with a natural rind. Teleme was first made by a Greek family in Pleasanton, and it evolved into a cheese that many immigrant communities in California craved. But then it more or less fell out of favor. "I got into making Teleme because there was a man in the Bay Area who asked me 'Why don't you have your father teach you to make Teleme because he's the only guy left alive who can make it?' I said, 'All right, I will,'" Franklin says.

So Franklin's father, Frank, taught him how to make Teleme, and Teleme soon became their signature cheese. "It's a challenging cheese to make, and that's what excites me," Franklin says.

Teleme, Franklin has learned, is a cheese that has similar counterparts around the world—not just the original Stracchino cheese. "The name, *Teleme,* is actually Turkish," Franklin says. "The Romanians also have a cheese that sounds like *Teleme.*"

While there was definite demand for Teleme in California, Franklin saw that there could be a good demand for it out on the East Coast. In 2005, Franklin sold his company, excluding his recipe for Teleme, and then moved out to Maine to make Teleme there under the auspices of his new company, Mid-Coast Cheese Company. But their stay in Maine was a bit short. Because his family missed California too much, just one year later they returned home, and, using the dairy facility at Cal Poly, Franklin continued to make Teleme.

Today, demand for his Teleme is as strong as ever. "It's a cheese that even people who don't care for cheese like," Franklin says. "It's a very mild cheese, and as it ages, it doesn't get that strong. It's also a very versatile cheese. It melts well so it's good for a pizza topping, but it's also good in polenta and a variety of dishes. It's also an excellent complement to figs, dates, and ripe fruit. My favorite way to eat it is on toasted French bread. Just the heat of the toast melts the Teleme."

Franklin has plans to make a goat's milk version, and he'd also like to make an American version of Taleggio. "I can't call it Taleggio, but I certainly will produce something similar," Franklin says.

POINT REYES FARMSTEAD CHEESE

14700 Highway 1

Point Reyes Station, CA 94956

4145-663-8880

www.pointreyescheese.com

COW'S MILK BLUE CHEESE

embers of the Giacomini family have been dairymen and -women in California for more than a century. In 1904, Tobias and Celestina Giacomini moved from the northern Italian Alps to Point Reyes. Their son, Waldo, continued the dairy tradition, and in 1959, their grandson, Bob, and his wife, Dean, purchased a farm just north of Point Reyes Station, almost abutting the Pacific Ocean.

After more than three decades of dairying, Bob and Dean wanted to retire and do something else so they talked it over with their four daughters—Diana, Jill Basch, Karen Howard, and Lynn Stray. "My sisters and I had moved away and gone to college," says Lynn. "None of us wanted to be involved in the animal side of the business. But it's 1997. My dad is sixty years old and he wants to step down, travel, and play golf, but what are we going to do with the farm?"

While Bob and Dean's daughters might not have wanted to work directly with the cows, they did have culinary interests. "We love to cook, and we love cheese," Lynn says. "The answer was right there."

Though Diana wasn't in a position to help out, Jill, Karen, and Lynn stepped up to carry on the family tradition. They decided to make one high-quality artisan cheese, and they decided on blue. "First of all, we love blue," Lynn says. "Looking around, nobody in the state of California was making a blue cheese. We decided we wanted to make a high-end table blue cheese."

The closest cheese to what they wanted to make was Maytag Blue. After further research and development they hired Monte McIntyre, who came from Iowa, where he had been making that wonderful cheese. But Monte and the family didn't create a replica of Maytag. Instead, they created an American original, Point Reyes Original Blue.

The blue cheese starts with the milk from 350 Holsteins, who get to graze on 700 acres. The pasture isn't just affected by the seasons and the fog. Because they are so close to the ocean, the salt flavors the grasses and thus the Marin County *terroir* shows up in the cheese. "Number one, it takes three daughters to make a good cheese," Bob says. "Also, because of the salt in the air, we don't have to add as much salt to our cheese."

Their award-winning cheese is Kosher-certified, and one third of their herd is certified as organic, too. The farm is constructing a methane digester to convert manure into electricity. "We have a land trust out here, and we very much support the Marin Agricultural Land Trust," Lynn says. "It has saved 60 farms in 25 years. It was the first land trust in the United States."

To continue to grow their business—and to open up the dairy to more visitors—the Giacomini family is constructing a new creamery on the farm. The new creamery will allow Monte and Rob Prokupek, assistant cheesemaker, more room to experiment with different cheeses; because of its nature, blue cheese must be kept completely separate from any other cheeses. The new facility will also have a classroom, which will allow the family to host cheese and culinary classes on the farm. With such continuing innovations, it's no wonder that the family creamery and farm received Outstanding Dairy of the Year award from the Sonoma County Fair in 2006.

Pug's Leap Farm

881 Dry Creek Road
Healdsburg, CA 95448
707-433-1021
pugsleap@comcast.net
Bloomy Rind Goat's Milk Cheeses

Every Saturday morning a crowd gathers around Pascal Destandau and his partner Eric Smith's booth at the Healdsburg Farmers Market. The couple offer up tastes from a tray with an array of delicate white goat's milk cheeses. These organic gems are almost too beautiful to cut into, let alone eat, but people eat them up, almost greedily.

Up until five years ago Pascal, a native of France, and Eric were virtually living worlds away. Pascal was working in pharmaceutical research and development in microbiology while Eric was working in architecture in San Francisco, when they decided they needed to completely change their urban lives. "I call it an epiphany, but everyone else says I had a midlife crisis," Pascal says.

The two moved out to Smith's grandparents' farm in Healdsburg, and it took them a year to get the farm and farmstead cheesemaking operation ready. They named the farm for their two dogs, Boy Pug and Oriane, who naturally leap around joyfully.

In 2004 they began making cheese the old-fashioned way. "I do everything by hand. We carry milk, don't pump, and have no holding tank," Pascal says.

They only milk their goats seasonally, too, and they also use 5-gallon milk pails instead of 10-gallon ones. "Agitation brings out the bad flavors in the milk," Pascal explains. "There's no mechanization whatsover. If you add that, you lose some of the quality."

Pascal and Eric are perfectionists in the best sense of the word, and they are passionate about eating and farming locally. Pascal learned how to make traditional goat's milk cheeses in France, but because of American pasteurization laws, he had to adapt. "He will take point one gram of this, point two grams of that," Eric says. "In France, they were working with raw milk, with what comes from the area, and here we put in cultures, but he's a master at that."

While Pascal might have to experiment with the different cultures to get the flavor profiles he so desires, what he doesn't experiment with is real rennet. "Ninety percent of cheese made in the United States is made with rennet produced by genetically modified organisms," Pascal says, adding that most of the microbial rennet comes from a microrganism that originally caused staphylococcus infections. "I think people need to know that. Real rennet is the way to go."

Smith is the master at taking care of their goats and keeping the farm running, using his background in architecture and design to create what they need to get the job done. Right now he's up before dawn to milk their 33 does. "We are at our absolute max," Eric says, adding that they're definitely not going to get any bigger, even as their demand grows.

"What we do cannot be scaled up," Pascal adds.

A woman comes up to their table and sees an article written about them that features a photo showing some very amiable goats. "That is why the cheese is so good," says the woman. "The goats really love you."

REDWOOD HILL FARM AND CREAMERY

2064 Highway 116 North, Building 1, Suite 130

Sebastopol, CA 95472

707-823-8250

www.redwoodhill.com

GOAT'S MILK CHEESES, YOGURT, AND KEFIR

Jennifer still knows all her goats by name. She visits with them with her brother, Scott, and sister, Sharon, both of whom work with her.

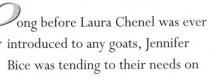ong before Laura Chenel was ever introduced to any goats, Jennifer Bice was tending to their needs on her family's Sonoma County farm. Her family had moved up from Los Angeles, and she and her siblings got into dairy goats through 4-H projects. "When my parents moved us to Sonoma County from the suburbs of Los Angeles, we felt like we were in solitary confinement," Jennifer recalls. "No sidewalks or neighbor kids to play with, so they got us animals of every type. The goats, of course, became the favorites, and that is still true today, and one of the reasons we have the business is for the goats!"

Those projects inspired a family business of selling goat's milk, and the Bice family opened up a farmstead creamery in 1968. As the oldest of 10 kids, Jennifer took the lead in helping her family with the dairy. "We milked before school," Jennifer says.

Just a decade later, Jennifer's love of goats led her and her late husband to take over the family's 10-acre farm and fresh milk-bottling business. Jennifer's initial business was just fresh milk, and in the 1970s goat's milk had gained traction in health food stores as a good alternative to cow's milk. "At the beginning, we felt like goat milk missionaries, and people would back up or start gagging when you mentioned 'goat' anything," Jennifer says.

In the 1980s she expanded the business to include goat's milk yogurt. "We actually came out with kefir [a cultured milk beverage], but then, people barely knew yogurt, let alone kefir, so we discontinued it and started with yogurt," Jennifer says. To promote both the milk and the yogurt, Jennifer and her family did demonstrations in grocery stores. It was during this time that people who normally wouldn't have touched goat's milk or yogurt began asking her if she made goat's milk cheese.

As consumers' interest in goat's milk cheese grew, Bice decided in 1988 to make chèvre, which they crafted at a nearby creamery. Two years later Jennifer opened a farmstead creamery. Then, in the 1990s, as demand for her cheese and yogurt grew, the farm outgrew its space. So Jennifer relocated the farm to a larger site, and then in 2003 she moved the creamery's operations to the former Vacu-dry Co. apple-processing plant on North Gravenstein Highway. As her company grew, she also began receiving milk from other nearby Sonoma goat dairies. Her brother, Scott, and sister, Sharon, also came back to work in the family business, with Scott managing the farm and Sharon heading up the communications and media relations.

Over the years she also expanded the lineup to include a raw milk feta, aged Tomme and Crottin, and the bloomy rind Camellia and Bucheret, all of which have received numerous awards from the American Cheese Society.

Most recently Jennifer and her cheesemakers reintroduced a goat's milk kefir and a new cheese, Gravenstein Gold. Kefir tastes like a creamy yogurt smoothie but it contains a different mix of cultures than regular yogurt. Gravenstein Gold is a washed rind cheese, and the wash used

SHARON BICE

Wheels of Gravenstein Gold age in the aging room.

to create its golden hues is made from a hard apple cider from local Gravenstein apple orchards.

"I think this cheese will be good for us," says Patty Beverly, cheese plant manager. "One thing that is notable is that its taste changes so much as it ages. It tastes very good young, but it is also good at the other end of the spectrum. From two weeks to ten weeks, it offers a full array of different flavors."

Though Jennifer has expanded her business greatly, she's never taken her focus away from the goats. Throughout the four decades since Redwood Hill's founding, she's worked hard to breed healthy goats. Her herd, which can be traced back to those original 4-H goats, has been exhibited at major shows and fairs and continues to win numerous national awards. Jennifer has had national champions in four of the five main goat breeds.

Jennifer has worked tirelessly to develop an excellent genetic program, and she has furnished stock to breeders across both North and South America. "We are committed to excellence in goat genetics, partly because of the holdover from 4-H and the fact that we like to show our dairy goats," she says. "When they win, other breeders want to buy their kids or breeding stock so that helps economically, but most important is that it is wonderful to work with beautiful animals. And yes, we do know all their names."

Jennifer has also judged at dairy goat competitions across the United States and Canada, and she has judged the American Dairy Goat Association National Show five times. With such hard work and dedication, it's no wonder that the American Humane Society chose her dairy to be the first goat dairy to receive the society's Humane Farm Animal Care's "Certified Humane Raised and Handled" label in 2003.

Besides her commitment to the goats, Jennifer also has an abiding love for the land. Redwood Hill Farm is a partner with the Sonoma Land Trust and a member of Co-op America, which works to keep lands intact. "We feel it is important for the quality of life and so that Sonoma County can remain an agricultural county," Jennifer says. "Buying local only works if you live somewhere where things can be grown."

Spring Hill Jersey Cheese Co.
Petaluma Creamery
Farm: 4235 Spring Hill Road
Creamery: 621 Western Avenue
Petaluma, CA 94952
707-762-3446
www.springhillcheese.com
Organic, Jersey Cow's Milk Cheeses; Some Goat's Milk Cheeses

Part maverick and part romantic, entrepreneur Larry Peter is a can-do kind of guy. In spite of, or especially, when people tell him he can't achieve something. "If they say I can't do it, I know I'm going to do it," Larry says.

Larry didn't grow up on a dairy, but his dad had dairy dreams. When Larry graduated from high school he had to go to work, and his entrepreneurial skills kicked in almost immediately. Sharing his dad's dream, Larry knew that if he was ever to own a dairy, he would need land, and land costs money. To save for his dream, he sold his car and rode his bike to work for five years.

Larry eventually got into rehabbing houses and real estate after working at a variety of jobs. By the time he was 27 years old, he was able to purchase 320 acres of farmland on Spring Hill Road. That initial purchase in 1986 was the start of his journey as a dairyman. Larry rehabbed the house—a classic Sears catalogue model—the farm, and then the land, prepping for his herd of Jersey cows. In 1998 he began producing cheese at his farmstead creamery, which he actually housed in trailers that used to be mobile school houses. "Those are portable school house number twenty-one and number twenty-two," Larry says. He also used a freezer from Santa Rosa College for an aging facility.

Larry grew his business slowly and steadily. Much of his cheese was—and still is—sold at local farmers' markets, and that's where his cheese developed a following. In 2004 he made the conversion to organic, but he took a huge jump in 2005. The Petaluma Creamery, which had been set up by Sonoma and Marin county dairy farmers in 1913, was shuttered by the Dairy Farmers of America in 2004. Larry hated to see such a Sonoma County landmark close, so he worked ardently to secure the funds to purchase the creamery. He moved some of his cheesemaking operations to the downtown Petaluma plant, and he's opened up the creamery store, which sells homemade ice cream and gourmet coffee, too.

"I love what I do," Larry says. "I want to educate people and keep agriculture alive in the county. I want people to know that agriculture is a dying pursuit, and we need to save it for the farmers. Let's do something so the next generation can do this."

Larry has plans to grow the creamery's business so that it remains a thriving presence in Petaluma. He also plans to continue milking his organic herd of Jerseys. As part of his desire to share what he loves, Larry does invite visitors to the creamery and farm, but the best time to visit his farm is in October, when he hosts The Great Peter Pumpkin Patch, a farm harvest festival that runs all month long. "About five thousand kids and their families come to see the farm, dig for potatoes, pick pumpkins, and milk cows," he says.

For anyone who dreams of starting a farmstead or artisan creamery, Larry recommends hard work and a positive attitude. "I don't give up," Larry says. "Persistence and passion can do anything."

CHAPTER 4

The Cheesemakers of
CENTRAL
CALIFORNIA

FISCALINI CHEESE COMPANY

7231 Covert Road

Modesto, CA 95358

209-545-5495

1-800-610-FARM

www.fiscalinicheese.com

COW'S MILK CHEESES—BANDAGE-WRAPPED CHEDDAR, AMERICAN ORIGINALS

Y ou could say milk flows through dairyman John Fiscalini's veins. His great-great-great grandfather was a dairy farmer and cheesemaker in Switzerland, and his grandfather founded the family farm in Modesto in 1914. Under his watch, John carefully increased the size of his Holstein herd from about 400 cows to now more than 1,000 to make it more viable; but a visit to his family's hometown in Lionza, in the Swiss Alps, also expanded his vision of what his farm could be.

That trip led him to think about the farmstead cheeses his ancestors crafted, and in 2000 he decided to install a little cheesemaking operation on his farm. He rescued a cheese vat from a scrap pile, added a boiler and a refrigerated aging room, and with the help of odds and ends, including an old ICEE penguin refrigerator that became a warming room, he put together a small cheese plant. Then, he set about learning the art of making cheese.

John stands inside the old aging room on his farm.

His first cheese, he decided, would be an Italian fontina. Shortly after making his first cheese, he encountered master cheesemaker Mariano Gonzalez. Mariano grew up making cheese in Paraguay. His uncle owned a dairy, but on the days it rained, the milk truck couldn't travel the winding roads, so Mariano helped his family craft cheese with the extra milk. Mariano later moved to Vermont, where a summer job at Shelburne Farms eventually led to him becoming the head cheesemaker

Cheese curds fly as cheesemakers begin the cheddaring process.

at this nationally renowned farmstead cheese operation. There, Mariano won many awards for his cheeses.

When Mariano met him, John was anxious for him to taste his first cheese, which he called fontina. "I was so proud of that cheese," John recalls. After tasting that cheese, Mariano told him, "This is a good cheese, but it's not fontina."

Instead, John had created an American original cheese, which he named San Joaquin Gold. Slightly saltier and firmer than a fontina, this beauty has a lovely gold color and a buttery taste. Its taste is so good that it has won many awards, including first place in the American Original Cow's Milk category in the 2008 American Cheese Society competition.

The cheese—and John's philosophy—impressed Mariano enough that he stayed, and he helped John further develop the small cheese plant and expand its line of cheeses. Because John's cows are so healthy and their milk is so high quality—it tests way, way above the federal standards, and the farm itself was the first farm certified for animal welfare by Validus, an organization that certifies humane treatment of animals—Mariano chose to craft cheeses from raw milk in an open vat, making the cheese by hand and in small batches. About 8 percent of Fiscalini's milk goes into the cheesemaking operations.

Mariano's cheeses at Fiscalini, like those he created at Shelbourne, won awards, but it wasn't until 2007 that the world literally woke up and took notice. Mariano had entered his 18-month-old bandaged cheddar in the World Cheese Awards in London, and for the first time in the competition's 20-year history, the best cheddar trophy left English soil: Fiscalini's cheddar became the first non-English cheese to win top honors in the Extra Mature Traditional Cheddar category.

Suddenly, magazines were calling the farmstead operation, and even congressmen were sending their congratulations. "We realized then what a big deal it was," Mariano says.

The accolades keep coming, and in just about every competition Fiscalini Cheese enters, it walks away with awards. And finally, later this year (2009) these award-winning cheeses will have a sparkling new cheesemaking facility and tasting room. The gorgeous quarters are expected to be completed in late 2009, allowing visitors a great chance not only to taste Mariano's amazing cheeses, but also to tour the farm, meet some of John's happy cows, and learn about dairy history. But visitors won't be able to see the old ICEE refrigerator, as it was discarded in the move.

Because people have asked for it, Fiscalini Cheese now makes some fresh Italian-style cheeses like mozzarella. They also make a cheese that honors John's dairy heritage: Lionza. Named after his ancestors' village, this Swiss-styled cheese is great for both fondues and snacking.

When he is not working with John, Mariano also helps Central American cheesemakers learn how to craft better cheeses, and he's taken several trips to work with them in developing better practices. "I just love what I do," says Mariano, who even named his dogs Cheddar and Feta. "By noon, you will have cheese, but at midnight, it was still inside the cow. It's really neat to watch the process."

Jonathan Van Ryn is one of the youngest cheesemakers in California.

BRAVO FARMS HANDMADE CHEESE

36005 Highway 99
Traver, CA 93673
559-897-4634
1-800-610-FARM
www.bravofarms.com

COW'S MILK CHEESES—CHEDDARS, GOUDA, EDAM, RACLETTE

If you're traveling along a certain stretch of Highway 99, a series of fun billboards might lead you to Bravo Farms' cheese factory and café in Traver. Antique signs advertising soft drinks greet visitors outside the wayside stop. Inside, there's not only a café—serving up 16 flavors of gourmet ice cream and delectable burgers—but there's also a quaint gift shop and a garden path, where you can dine in the sunshine or shade, and can also visit some chickens in a coop.

In addition, you can view cheesemaking from a window, and there are even tours offered daily. While the café is a newer addition, Bravo Farms has a longer history in the Central Valley. The farm was started by Bill Boersma, a fourth-generation dairyman, in 1979. He started making cheese about 12 years ago, and he became partners with Jonathan Van Ryn just 2 years ago.

Jonathan is perhaps one of the youngest cheesemakers in the country, having studied the dairy art at Cal Poly; his grandfather was a dairyman. "I thought I'd study the (cow) side of dairy science, and I got into cheesemaking," Jonathan says. "I like that my job changes every day, and there are a million different aspects to it."

The café and small factory used to be a fruit stand and cider-making operation that dates back six decades. They revamped the property and installed three vats, as well as the restaurant and the garden. To make the cheese, they decided to use raw milk from the Jersey cows on Jonathan's uncle's farm. "If you look at blocks of cheese made from Jerseys and those made from Holsteins, the blocks of cheese made with Jersey milk are more buttery—you can actually see it because they're more yellow in color," Jonathan says.

Jonathan, Bill, and their team of five other cheesemakers craft a variety of cheddars, including some delicious flavors like chipotle and sage, but they also make a traditional, cloth-bound cheddar they call Silver Mountain. This cheddar is rubbed in olive oil and aged for at least nine months, and it has a bold flavor.

They also make an Edam called the Tulare Cannonball. "We used a five-hundred-year-old recipe that Bill found in a Dutch library," Jonathan says. The Cannonball looks just like, well, a cannonball, big and round and packing a punch of flavor.

Their newest cheese is a Swiss raclette, which has been selling out along with a Gouda and a white cheddar, too. Their cheeses not only sell well, but they also have earned numerous awards at competitions. "We don't sell cheese based on price so we'd better have the best-quality product out there," Jonathan says. "People are always amazed at how good our cheese is, and at the farmers' market, it sells itself."

FAGUNDES OLD-WORLD CHEESE

8700 Fargo Avenue

Hanford, CA 93230

559-582-2000

ALSO

FARIA'S RANCH MARKET

8606 Avenue 280

Visalia, CA 93277

559-651-0994

www.oldworldcheese.com

COW'S MILK CHEESES—PORTUGUESE,
HISPANIC, JACK, AND MORE; AGED GOAT'S MILK CHEESES

Fagundes might be the only cheesemaker in the world that also grows kiwis.

In the late 1990s the California Milk Advisory Board held a series of seminars, inviting state dairyman to consider adding farmstead cheese production to their farms. "We were one of the ones who bit," says John Fagundes, master cheesemaker and longtime dairyman.

John's family has a long dairy and cheesemaking history that spans two countries. In the late 19th century, Isabel Fagundes became widowed, and she made cheese to support her family on the Azores Islands in Portugal. In 1886, her son John immigrated to America, and in 1909 his son, John II, moved from Providence, Rhode Island, to California, where he purchased a dairy in Hanford. The family farm still stands there today.

John IV remembers his own grandmother making cheese in the kitchen using coffee cans. After he decided he wanted to make cheese, he and his family headed to the Azores for inspiration, specifically to the village of Larale on the island of Sao Jorge, where his great-grandmother made cheese. "The first cheese we tried to make was a St. Jorge, a traditional

Portuguese cheese," John says. "But the cheese was creamier and milder so we called it St. John."

John did develop a St. Jorge cheese, and both his St. John and St. Jorge cheeses have won numerous awards, including Best Hispanic and Portuguese-Style Cheese from the American Cheese Society. He also makes a line of Monterey Jack cheeses, and his Hanford Jack has taken top honors at the American Cheese Society, too. "Since we're from California, we felt we'd have to do a jack," John says.

Besides the Portuguese and jack cheeses, John also makes some Hispanic cheeses, and he makes some aged goat's milk cheeses, too. "Last year was the first year we did some goat's milk cheeses," John says. "We get the goat milk from a neighbor's farm."

All the milk for the jack, Portuguese, and Hispanic cheeses comes from the family herd of 800 Holsteins. Because they don't use all their milk for their cheese production, they get to choose the milk that works best for their cheeses. "We have the luxury of selecting the milk and even the stage of lactation for our cheese," John says. "We like middle lactation best, when the cows are less stressed."

Their herd of cows (which do not receive any bovine growth hormones at all) and the farm are run by John's father, John III, and his brother, Bruce. John's oldest daughter, Brittany, who is a senior at Cal Poly, is majoring in dairy science with a minor in history and journalism. His youngest daughter, Mary, is still determining her field of study at junior college. The family also has a kiwi farm, part of which is organic, and about one third of all the organic kiwis at market throughout the United States come from their farm. "The cows do eat some kiwis," John admits.

RINCONADA DAIRY AND BED AND BREAKFAST

4680 West Pozo Road

Santa Margarita, CA 93453

805-438-5667

www.rinconadadairy.com

AGED GOAT'S AND SHEEP'S MILK, AMERICAN ORIGINALS

Tucked away in the rolling hills of San Luis Obispo County, in the shadow of Rinconada Peak, is a gorgeous 52-acre ranch. The ranch, which is home to goats, sheep, pigs, chickens, cats, and two friendly border collies, is the culmination of a dream that Christine and Jim Maguire held for many years.

The two globe-trotting professionals got a taste of the country life in England. "We lived

Christine's goats greet her.

for a year in a farmhouse on Devon, and that's when we knew we really wanted a more country life," Christine says. "We had lived in San Francisco, Seattle, Montreal, and London."

Their country life began on a small, 1½-acre farm with some chickens and a large garden, and then their first goat arrived in the early 1990s. "Sadie Kendall (of Kendall Cheese Company) gave me a goat, and that was the end of that," Christine says. Then in 1998 they got their first sheep, and that decided their future. The following year they purchased their lovely ranch, restoring the buildings on the prop-

When they're not accompanying her around the farm, Christine's dogs live the good life.

erty and building a creamery on the farm.

In 2001 some college students from Cal Poly helped Christine as their major senior project by sending out a survey to 300 wineries, cheese shops, and restaurants, asking them if they would be interested in carrying a sheep's milk cheese. "Over fifty percent responded, saying 'Sheep's milk cheese? You bet,'" Christine says. "They (the students) said 'You can do this thing.'" The following year their creamery was up and running, and Christine was making her sheep's milk and goat's milk cheeses. Their creamery, along with Bellwether Farms, is one of only two sheep's milk creameries in the entire state.

Unlike many creameries, which start with fresh cheeses before moving into aged varieties, Christine started—and has stayed—with raw milk, aged cheeses. "I've never pasteurized. It's always been raw milk, and I knew I wanted to start with semihard cheeses," Christine says. "The cheeses are inspired by our time in England, and by our travels in Italy, France, and Spain, but it started with living in England."

Christine makes two sheep's milk cheeses and one mixed milk cheese of both sheep's and goat's milk, and her hands-on attention has paid off. She's received several awards, including a first place at the American Cheese Society in her category in 2005, and many chefs throughout California use her cheeses.

Tending to the farm—the land and the animals—is Christine and Jim's all-consuming passion. "It's what we do," Christine says. What they do is beyond what most ranchers do. They use no pesticides, herbicides, or artificial fertilizers, and their animals aren't given any antibiotics or hormones. They also carefully breed their sheep and goats, and they make sure that they are well cared for. Some of their lambs and pigs are sold to local chefs. "Everything we do here is hands on—either by me or Jim, and we try to be, as much as we can, self-sufficient," Christine says. "The whey isn't wasted. It feeds the pigs."

Their peaceful ranch isn't just a fun place to visit or to purchase cheese. It's also a bed and breakfast, and Christine, who is a graduate of the Natural Gourmet Institute in New York City, cooks up farm-fresh breakfasts using eggs from her chickens, pears from her trees, and vegetables from her garden. One morning it might be French toast with homemade pomegranate syrup and sautéed apples; another morning it might be a fluffy omelet with homemade salsa. And, of course, there's cheese, too.

THREE SISTERS FARMSTEAD CHEESE

24163 Road 188
Lindsay, CA 93247
559-562-2132
www.threesisterscheese.com
COW'S MILK, AMERICAN ORIGINALS

Marisa, a fourth-generation dairywoman, shows off her wheels in the new aging room.

*M*arisa Simoes grew up on a large dairy farm in the San Joaquin Valley in Tulare County, which just happens to be the biggest dairy region in the country. Her father, Rob Hilarides, a third-generation dairy farmer, used to joke with her and her two younger sisters, Lindsay and Hannah, about making cheese. None of his daughters took him seriously until Marisa returned home after a year of college in Los Angeles.

At age 19, in 1999, she decided that she was more of a country girl at heart, and she and her father took a cheesemaking course together at California Polytechnic State University San Luis Obispo. After taking the class, she and her family decided that if they were going to make cheese, they had to make a cheese they liked—in case they got stuck with a batch that didn't sell. The whole family took a trip up to San Francisco, and they spent a night in a hotel room tasting cheeses.

"We sat down as a family and discussed what we liked and what we could make," Marisa says. They discovered they liked the harder, nuttier, aged cheeses, and for their debut cheese they decided to develop an Italian-inspired variety, which they called Serena.

Because they didn't have a cheese plant on their farm, they went to Bravo Farms. "Bill

Jersey cows sun themselves just outside the creamery doors.

(Boersma) was kind enough to let us use his cheesemaking room after hours," Marisa says. A wheel from that very first batch took third place in the American Originals category at the American Cheese Society competition. That was back in 2000, and they were suddenly in the cheesemaking business, with upscale grocers approaching Simoes, wanting to sell her cheese. The smooth and nutty cheese boasts complex flavors and a creamy, yellow color that comes from the richness of the milk from their Jersey herd.

In 2004, Marisa and her father built a small cheesemaking plant on their farm. Though the family farms a herd of 8,000 cattle, with most of the milk supplying the large Hilmar Cheese Company, the cheesemaking operations remain definitively farmstead in both size and quality. All the cheese is made by hand in small batches, and it is aged on the farm in special cellars.

Though they were content just to make their award-winning Serena, in 2005 they created their second cheese: Serenita. They didn't set out to make a new cheese, but one day in the middle of making cheese they experienced a power outage, so they had to improvise and use different techniques to make the cheese, which came out a bit milder and sweeter. "This came about as a mistake," Marisa says.

But it was a delicious mistake, and that year it took first place in the American Originals category of the American Cheese Society competition. "You can taste the *terroir* of the valley in our cheeses," Marisa says. "We grow almost all our feed, which our cows eat, and we use California olive oil (to rub on the cheese)."

CHAPTER 5

The Cheesemakers of
SOUTHERN
CALIFORNIA

BUBALUS BUBALIS

18207 South Broadway

Gardena, CA 90248

310-515-0500

www.realmozzarella.com

WATER BUFFALO MOZZARELLA AND RICOTTA

A cheesemaker makes fresh mozzarella.

Authentic mozzarella isn't the shredded stuff found in bags in most supermarkets. It's not even, really, found in all Italian grocery stores. The difference is in the milk. The most authentic mozzarella is called mozzarella *di bufala* or mozzarella made with the milk of water buffalos, and because it is a fresh cheese, it's harder to import so not all gourmet or Italian grocers carry such delicacies.

Fortunately for mozzarella lovers everywhere, wife and husband team Grazia Perrella and Hanns Heick offer an alternative to this rare import—a domestically crafted, authentic mozzzarella *di bufala*. "It's really the flavor," Hanns says. "It's just richer in flavor."

The flavor started in 1998 when Virgil Cicconi purchased a small herd of water buffalo from Florida (the herd originated in Italy) and moved it to California. Hanns and Grazia took over the company, Bubalus Bubalis in 2002. Hanns has a background in wine exportation while Grazia comes from a family that has had generations of mozzarella makers in the Naples area of Italy. Hanns said the taste of the mozzarella convinced him and his wife to buy the company.

"It's kind of one of those things where you like the product, and you start making it," Hanns says. "It's a pleasure to have a product that you don't have to praise too much. It praises itself, and people enjoy it. It's a pleasure to make."

They kept the name, Bubalus Bubalis, when they took over the company. The name actually is the Latin or scientific name for Asian water buffalo. Not only is it accurate, but the name has a lyrical, fun quality that makes it as memorable as the cheese.

Hanns and Grazia moved the herd from its initial pastures of Chino to Bangor, which is located in eastern Butte County, north of Sacramento. Butte County grows a lot of rice, and water buffalo love to eat rice straw. "They are really gentle creatures," Hanns says. "They are very curious, and they like to swim or roll around in mud piles."

But while they moved the herd to be closer to the herd's favorite food source, they kept the factory's plant in Gardena. The small plant employs only a handful of employees, and it's located in a nondescript industrial block, close to Los Angeles.

Because mozzarella is a cheese that tastes better when it is fresher, it is Hanns and Grazia's goal to get the mozzarella to their customers within just three to four days of its making. "We are try-ing to come as close as possible to give our customers a fresh cheese," Hanns says. "If you import fresh moz-zarella *di bufala,* that's a long distance for fresh cheese to travel. An Italian would not be happy with importing. The idea is, because it is called fresh, the closer you come to production, the better the flavor."

Not only are Italians and gourmet foodies alike enjoying these domestically crafted cheeses, but so are those who are lactose intolerant. Because of the nature

Bubalus bubalis *is the scientific name for water buffalo.*

of water buffalo milk and the process of creating fresh mozzarella, the resulting cheese is virtually lactose-free while at the same time boasting a high content of calcium, protein, and other good stuff. "This is a full meal. It contains everything you need," Hanns says. "We have some customers who can't consume other dairy products, but they can eat our cheese."

Like any good mozzarella makers, Hanns and Grazia make ricotta, too. "It makes a good cheesecake," Hanns says. "Just add a little lemon and sugar, and it's unbelievable."

Vito is a third-generation Italian cheesemaker.

GIOIA CHEESE CO.

1605 Potrero Avenue
South El Monte, CA 91733
626-444-6015
FRESH MOZZARELLA AND BURRATA

*V*ito Girardi's grandfather, Antonio, and father, Frank, were both cheesemakers, and he grew up in Bari, Italy, a city in the Puglia region. "My father dragged me into the cheese business when I was fourteen years old," Vito says. "I'm the only one in my family who stayed in the same business."

That is the business of making cow's milk mozzarella, and specifically *burrata*, the exceptionally decadent variety of mozzarella. *Burrata,* which was invented in the Puglia region, is a special type of cow's milk mozzarella. It is basically a thinly spun fresh mozzarella shell that is filled with cream and bits of mozzarella curds. When you cut into it, it just oozes creamy goodness.

Vito loves *burrata,* and when his maternal grandparents (not the ones who made mozzarella) moved to California, he and his family eventually followed. Vito and his family moved in 1992, and in 1993 he started the Gioia Cheese Company in South El Monte. "I introduced specialty *burrata* to the United States," Vito says. "Before, no one knew what it was, but it has become quite popular."

Vito uses his family's old, traditional recipe, but more than the recipe, it relies on a technique that's been handed down in his family. "There's no machine that can make specialty *burrata,*" Vito says. "Because it's made by hand, there's a limited production."

Back when Vito started making mozzarella and *burrata,* he had to stretch the curd by hand. "The thing is, the water's very hot, and you burn your hands when you get started," Vito says. "Today, you don't have to do that (for regular mozzarella). Thank God they invented a machine for that!"

Since he started, Vito's business has expanded. Besides *burrata,* he also makes other versions of fresh mozzarella, along with mascarpone and ricotta. He hasn't taken a vacation in more than a decade. "I don't get a vacation, but at least give me a weekend," Vito says, explaining that he must take his weekends off. "For thirty-five years, my father never took a vacation, either."

His wife, Monica, and son, Frank, work with him, and he now employs about 20 people. "Now, my son will be the fourth generation," Vito says. "When we started, we were making only four hundred pounds of *burrata* in a year. Now, we make ten thousand pounds in one week. I know there's a lot of potential for more. We really keep busy with this cheese."

Vito appreciates that his family's business has grown, but he believes that incremental growth is better. "It's growing day by day, but I like to grow slow. I can keep control," he says. "It's grown from word of mouth, from one customer to another. I love cheese, and I eat cheese every day. I always tell my wife I'll never starve because I can always make my own cheese."

SOLEDAD GOATS

6501 Backus Road
Mojave, CA 93501
661-824-4514
FRESH GOAT'S MILK CHEESES

Julian and Carol talk with customers at one of the many farmers' markets they go to each week.

For Julian and Carol Pierce, it was love at first scouring. Both dairy folk, Julian was a British preruminate specialist while Carol ran a dairy in Pennsylvania. "We met over scouring calves," Carol says. "I was a confirmed bachelor," Julian says, adding that he fell hard for Carol.

That was 15 years ago, and after they fell head over heels for each other, she ended up following Julian back to England.

Back in England, they began getting into goat's milk and goat's milk cheeses. They started out with just the goats and goat's milk, and at their place in Dorset they had 1,200 goats. Then, Carol's creativity was sparked by the idea of making cheese.

Carol's cheeses won gold awards at the World Cheese Awards in London, as well as the Perpetual Cup at the Frome Cheese Show in England, and both she and Julian loved what they were doing. "I just had these different ideas for making cheese," Carol says. "I had these ideas for flavors like lavender and lemon or salmon and dill and flavors that were difficult."

But the cost of doing business in England, coupled with not-so-nice weather, led them to think that maybe they'd be better off in a warmer climate. They looked all over the United States, and many people invited them to come to Northern California. Instead, though, they chose Southern California, and they ended up settling on a farm at the foot of Soledad

An artful display in Soledad Goats' farmers' market booth.

Mountain. "We thought, there's no one making goat's milk cheese in Southern California, and we found a place near Mojave," Carol says. "With a city the size of Los Angeles not having any goat cheeses, that's why we decided to move here."

That was in 2006, and they've settled right into the agriculture business outside of Los Angeles. Every week you'll find them at dozens of farmers' markets throughout the region, from the Hollywood Farmers' Market to the Antelope Valley Winery market. Their farm is scaled down quite a bit from Dorset's size, down to 150 goats. "We grow our own herbs and milk our goats, and we source other ingredients from organic small farmers," Carol says.

They handle the milk very gently in both pasteurization and cheesemaking. When they were in England they learned how different handling techniques could adversely affect the milk. There they had two different vats—one square shaped and one circular. The square vat was too rough on the milk, and "you could smell Billy," Carol says. "It broke the proteins in the milk as soon as it hit the walls, and it just destroyed the milk."

Besides gentle handling, Carol uses 14 different herbs and spices as flavorings for her fresh chèvre. She also preserves some chèvre buttons in extra virgin olive oil. "The olive oil acts as a preservative," she says.

With their new farm, Carol and Julian have plans to open a more formal visitors' center, as they love to have people visit. "We love to have people meet our goats," Carol says. And they also love to have people meet their rescue horses, dogs, cats, and chickens.

Their love for each other is only enhanced by their love for their animals. They basically take in animals, especially goats, that others won't, and they take care of their "retired nannies." "These girls worked for us so we can't say to them 'Oops, now you're done,'" Carol says.

Back in England one of Carol's favorite goats had a bald head, no teeth, and was prone to bloody noses. She was the type of goat that many farmers would have gotten rid of. Instead, she turned out to be a good milker and a great mother, and she used to get piggyback (or rather, goatback) rides on Carol's shoulders. "She was such a good nanny," Carol says. "If we get depressed or fed up, we just go out to see the goats."

"It's such great fun," adds Julian.

WINCHESTER CHEESE COMPANY

32605 Holland Road
Winchester, CA 92596
951-926-4239
www.winchestercheese.com

COW'S MILK CHEESES—GOUDAS

*L*ess than an hour's drive from San Diego, near Temecula wine country, you can visit Winchester Cheese Company. Winchester, besides making incredible and authentic Gouda, boasts the honor of being the southernmost cheesemaking facility in California.

Winchester's venerable history starts with its founder, Jules Wesselink and his wife, Corrie, who are originally from Haarlem, Holland. Jules and his wife moved to California in 1951, and after owning various dairies throughout the Golden State, they bought land and built a dairy in Winchester in 1978. Their property coincidentally happened to be located on the aptly named Holland Road.

Jules hadn't planned on making cheese, but in 1995 he and Corrie returned to Holland to celebrate it's 50th anniversary of liberation from the Nazis. "I stayed with relatives who had a cheese dairy and, for the heck of it, I just learned to make cheese," Jules says. Jules's cousin, Frank Olfdhoorn, taught him how to make cheese, using his family's recipes that have been handed down for 700 years, and Jules bought a cheesemaking kit in Holland. When he returned home, he made two baby wheels of Gouda and let them age for two months. "Then we tasted it, and it was delicious, and a friend asked me, 'Can you make me two wheels?'" Jules says.

So Jules made him 2 wheels, and then, when a cheesemaker in Escondido quit, he purchased 30 molds, so he made 30 small wheels. "Then my wife, Corrie, and my daughter Valerie went to the farmers' market in Temecula and sold them, and they sold very good,"

Jules says. "Now, we're shipping cheese all over the place. My first commercial customer was Emeril (LaGasse), and we used to ship two cheeses every month to New Orleans."

Jules's real *boere kaas* or farmstead Goudas, which are made from raw milk, range from the mild aged, which is only aged two months, to the super aged, which is aged for a year or more. They also have a medium, aged for three to four months, a sharp, aged for six to eight months, and several flavors of Gouda, including jalapeño and cumin. Every year their Goudas win awards, and they've racked up wins at the American Cheese Society and the World Cheese Awards in London. "Our number-one seller is the medium-aged Gouda, but our flagship is our super aged," says Jeff Smoot, general manager. "People also love our jalapeño."

Today Jules, at age 80, still heads up the family farm, but the cheese is made by his daughter Valerie and son-in-law David Thomas. His daughter Pauline and son-in-law David Thornton also are involved, as is his son Leo and daughter-in-law Betty. The cheese plant has also expanded quite a bit, hiring on an additional cheesemaker, Marnie Clarke, who, at 24, is one of the youngest cheesemakers in the county. They have plans to add a few new cheeses to their lineup of Goudas. "It's just that there's so much tradition, it's hard to break with it," Marnie says.

"New cheeses generate new interest," Jeff adds. "Even when we make a new flavor of Gouda, people are drawn to it."

People are also drawn to Winchester's interesting building. Not only does Winchester have the youngest cheesemaker in the state working in the southernmost cheese plant, but that plant is a story in itself.

Winchester is, as far as is known, the only cheese plant to be housed in a trailer that has a valid license plate. "What prevented us from putting a building on site is that someone saw an endangered kangaroo rat on the property," Jeff says. "You have to have a special permit to have a building, and it was going to be a fortune," Jules explains. "I was at a livestock auction, and I saw these trailers that move meats, so I bought one of those and I started making cheese in it."

The truck, which still has its wheels, is still registered with the California Department of Motor Vehicles, but now it's not one truck, it is ten trucks connected together. "I always take people outside to see the actual license plate because it's current," says Marnie. "When I first came to Winchester, I didn't realize I was in a truck all day for the first couple of weeks."

"It doesn't feel like you're in a truck. It's pretty big," Jeff adds. "And none of us has ever seen a kangaroo rat. We've got cats and coyotes and snakes, but there's not a rat to be seen."

CHAPTER 6

Other Dairy Masters of
CALIFORNIA
(Including Ice Cream, Milk, Yogurt, and Crème Fraîche)

HUMBOLDT CREAMERY

572 Highway 1

Fortuna, CA 95540

707-725-6182

www.humboldtcreamery.com

ORGANIC COW'S MILK ICE CREAM AND ICE CREAM TREATS

The oldest dairy cooperative in California, Humboldt Creamery, got its start when a group of 150 dairymen got together in 1929 and put in their dime's share. "That's what built this factory here, and originally they made milk, cheese, butter, and related dairy products," says Jeff Sussman, national sales and marketing manager.

Up until the 1970s the co-op made these products, some under the Challenge Dairy Label, but in the 1970s and 1980s they created the Humboldt Creamery brand. Then in the early 1990s they converted the butter production into ice cream, and now the company makes ice cream, milk, and milk products. Today, the company is owned by about 60 dairymen, most of whom are third- or fourth-generation farmers, and they average about 250 cows per dairy, which is quite small for California. Half the company's milk is certified organic, and none of the farmers use bovine growth hormone.

"We are one of the largest suppliers of organic milk on the West Coast," says Jeff. "Organic seemed like a natural fit to our method of dairy farming."

Much of the ice cream is sold under the Humboldt Creamery brand, but the company also co-packs for some major national retailers (including one membership warehouse that is known for its good, in-store ice cream). Their ice cream is sold across the country and also exported to Mexico and Peru, and they have plans to possibly expand to the Pacific Rim and throughout South America.

The company's secret to success? The cows. "All our dairy farmers in Humboldt County are pasture-based farms," Jeff says. "These are the happy cows. They are a mix of Jerseys and

Holsteins. One of our core beliefs is to maintain sustainable agriculture and maintain integrity in our product. We care about the earth."

On average, their cows each get about an acre of pasture to graze on, and they tend to live longer, better lives—an average of 8 to 12 years, versus the 3 to 5 years of a feedlot cow. Indeed, if you step off the plane and drive away from the Eureka Airport, you'll see green pastures with contented bovines. If there aren't redwood trees in sight, there are pastures filled with joyful cows found throughout the county. In the past, the American Humane Society has certified the brand for its good treatment of their cows.

"We have one of the highest fat contents in milk in the entire United States," Jeff says. "We believe that pasture grazing and grass feeding is a natural way to produce milk."

Their organic milk is both sweet and satisfying, but what tastes even better is their ice cream. "We use really good ingredients," Jeff says. "We use pure Madagascar vanilla, we use really good chocolate, and our ice cream has sixteen percent butterfat."

Flavors range from the more exotic—marionberry cobbler and espresso chip—to the typical strawberry and chocolate; Humboldt Creamery also makes frozen dessert treats like cherry-pineapple super treats. "The super treats are just killer," Jeff says.

KENDALL CHEESE COMPANY

P.O. Box 686
Atascadero, CA 93422
805-466-7252
www.kendallfarmscremefraiche.com
CRÈME FRAÎCHE

Sadie Kendall first started making cheese in the early 1970s. "It was a hobby," she says. "I was working on a philosophy degree, and I had moved to Los Angeles. I was working on my degree with the intention of going to law school. Where I lived was known for agriculture, and I liked to cook."

While studying for her degree, Sadie worked as a legal secretary for a firm that was located not too far away from the Beverly Hills Cheese Shop. She would head to the shop on her lunch break, and that inspired her. "I got a backyard goat, and I decided, coupled with my interest in cooking, to try to make cheese," Sadie says. "In my last semester I took a food science class, and I said to myself 'I don't want to be a lawyer, I want to be a cheesemaker.'"

Sadie finished her philosophy degree, but instead of law school she pursued graduate school at Cal Poly to study dairy science. In 1981, she and her husband, Jeffrey Sicha, found an old dairy in Atascadero. They had to restore the plumbing and electricity, but then they were in business. Starting with a herd of about 30 Nubian goats, Sadie began to make cheese commercially. One of the cheeses she made was *chèvrefeuille,* which is a goat's milk Camembert; it literally means "goat leaf" in French. (It is the French word for honeysuckle, too.) She also made a goat's milk Stilton cheese, but in 1985 she started making making crème fraîche.

The crème fraîche evolved from her experiments with cow's milk. Along with her herd of goats, which had grown considerably from the original 30, she had 2 Jersey cows and 1 Guernsey cow. She used their milk to feed the goat kids because the goat's milk was more valuable to cheese production; she also crafted a cultured butter and a Camembert that was made from 50 percent cow's milk and 50 percent goat's milk. "On one of my trips to San Francisco, to deliver cheese to the Oakville Grocery, I picked up a container of crème fraîche because I had never heard of it," Sadie says. "I liked it, and decided that I would like to have that for my own table. But knowing where I lived, I knew I would have to make it myself."

So Sadie set out to determine how to make crème fraîche, and she shared her experiments with a local chef. "I discovered that I had something because nobody was making crème fraîche in California," Sadie says. By 1987 she was selling her crème fraîche to local chefs and to stores. Around the same time that her crème fraîche production was growing, she and her husband were starting to experience problems with getting the necessary help for the goats. "My passion was for making cheese so we decided to sell the herd," Sadie says.

So by 2000 they sold the herd of goats, with the intention of purchasing milk for cheesemaking. But she couldn't find enough quality goat's milk to purchase. "Without the Nubian milk, I couldn't make the *chèvrefeuille,* and while fresh chèvre is lovely, it just isn't what I had in mind," Sadie says. "By that time the crème fraîche was doing quite nicely so we thought, why don't we try to make a go of it with just the crème fraîche? It worked."

In focusing on the crème fraîche, Sadie worked out a perfect formula to get the crème fraîche exactly right. But after setting up the right parameters, Sadie channeled her creativity into experimenting with crème fraîche in the kitchen. "The applications of using it are just astounding," Sadie says.

Crème fraîche, she discovered, is an almost magical ingredient for sauces. Instead of reducing cream, which can sometimes fall apart into butter and oil, crème fraîche doesn't need to be reduced—it's naturally thick and creamy. Also, it is good when blended with whipping cream. "If you take equal amounts of whipping cream and crème fraîche, you will discover that the crème fraîche will give you twice the volume of foam, and the foam is finer and denser, and it doesn't collapse the way ordinary whipping cream does," Sadie says. "Also, you can store it in your refrigerator for up to a week."

This crème chantilly pairs beautifully with fresh fruits, but crème fraîche also works wonderfully with savory flavors as well. "It is a beautiful carrier of aromatics," Sadie says. "It's absolutely exquisite. If you stir fresh herbs into the crème fraîche and then let it sit for a couple of hours in the refrigerator, the herbs perfume the crème fraîche, and you can have these scented sauces that are just divine."

Sadie is happy that her business has turned out so well, but she wouldn't recommend that others start out the way she did. "It was all passion," she says. "It was wonderful so, of course, people bought it. We knew nothing about business, just that (our cheese) was wonderful, and it was just that we were very lucky that there were enough other people out there, chefs in particular, who had gone to Europe and discovered good food."

Gravenstein Gold tastes delicious with figs.   CREDIT: SHARON BICE

LEFT: *This wedding cake is made of Humboldt Fog cheese.*

ABOVE: *Harley Farms chèvre logs come in four flavors: pepper, chives, dill, and plain.*

ABOVE: *The cheeses at Cypress Grove Chèvre are every bit as delicious as they look.*

RIGHT: *Harley Farms chèvre is as beautiful as it is delicious.*

Redwood Hill's gorgeous goat's milk cheeses go well with crusty bread. PHOTO: SHARON BICE

RIGHT: *Harley Farms' beautiful wheels of chèvre studded with fresh flowers come in extra-large sizes, too.*

Laura Chenel's Chèvre tastes absolutely divine tossed with fresh vegetables in a refreshing salad.

LALOO'S GOAT'S MILK ICE CREAM COMPANY

3190 Eastman Lane
Petaluma, CA 94952
707-763-1491
www.goatmilkicecream.com
GOAT'S MILK ICE CREAM AND FROZEN YOGURT

It was yoga that led Laura Howard to the creation of the world's first goat's milk ice cream company. A busy Hollywood film executive, Laura was studying yoga, and as she progressed on her path of study, she went on a cleansing diet in which she wasn't allowed to eat any cow's milk, caffeine, or alcohol.

The caffeine and the alcohol were a lot easier to give up than the dairy, as she consumed pints of Ben & Jerry's ice cream on a regular basis. Not wanting to give up dairy but desiring to follow the diet, she further researched it, and she discovered that goat's milk was allowed.

But since no one made goat's milk ice cream, Laura began experimenting in her kitchen, using her grandmother's old-fashioned ice cream churner and a 1940s-era *Joy of Cooking.* After trying her own ice cream, Howard didn't miss Ben & Jerry's anymore. The taste—and the fact that goat's milk ice cream is lower in both fat and calories than cow's milk ice cream—led Howard to realize she was onto something wonderful. "It tastes just like regular ice cream, but it's better for you," Laura says. "It is slow cooked and slow churned, more like custard or gelato."

Laloo's goat's milk ice cream uses the freshest and finest ingredients.

CARRYON COMMUNICATIONS, INC., KRIS ELLENBERG

That was the start of Laura's journey away from film and into food. The next step in her path was her introduction to the Slow Food Movement. While on location filming an independent movie in Tuscany, Howard met a photographer, Douglas Gayeton, who was there photographing a series called "Slow: Life in a Tuscan Town." Laura fell in love with Gayeton and Slow Food, and she ended up marrying Gayeton. "I felt I had discovered a new world order, and I knew that food was going to play a prominent role in my next chapter," Laura says.

In 2004 Laura left the film industry and decided to take her discovery to the next level, founding Laloo's (pronounced Lay-Looz) Goat's Milk Ice Cream Company in Petaluma. The name Laloo was her childhood nickname. "I got out of my old career to put something beautiful in the world and to make people happier," Laura says. "And nothing makes people happier than ice cream."

Not only is her premium ice cream lower in calories and fats, but people who are lactose intolerant can eat it because goat's milk is more easily digested than cow's milk. Healthful probiotics are also added as another benefit, and part of the proceeds from the ice cream are donated to the Waterkeeper Alliance to help protect watersheds from pollution. Her ice cream is also certified as Free Farm Humane and Kosher.

Her ice cream comes in bold and fun flavors like Strawberry Darling, which boasts real strawberries and swirls of balsamic reduction; Black Mission Fig, which is chock-full of delicious figs; and Cherries Tuilerie, a decadent cherry confection named after her two-year-old daughter. "I just took a lot of my favorite things and put them in ice cream," Laura says.

St. Benoît Yogurt

1796 Pepper Road
Petaluma, CA
530-400-4701
www.stbenoit.com
Email: benoit@stbenoit.com

Jersey Cow's Milk Yogurt

When Benoît de Korsak moved to northern California from France, the one taste he couldn't find anywhere was French-style yogurt. "The quality of yogurt is quite different in France, and in France we eat a lot more yogurt," Benoît says. "I see a lot of artisanal French-style cheese here, but none of the French yogurt."

French yogurt is lusher, thicker, and less sweet than American yogurts, and unlike American yogurts, it doesn't have any thickeners or stabilizers. Even looking far and wide, Benoît couldn't find any suitable substitutes for his craving. So, with the help of his brother David, he founded St. Benoît Yogurt in 2003, beginning production the following year. The name refers not to him, but to Saint Benoît or Saint Benedict, who founded several monastic communities that became known for their artisan foods, especially cheeses and wines. The name honors the heritage from Saint Benedict. The yogurt is made in very small batches, and often his entire family—wife Kristine, eight-year-old daughter Emma, five-year-old son Pierre, and three-year-old daughter Charlotte—helps out.

The whole milk used to make the yogurt comes from an all-Jersey herd, and it is made with a French yogurt culture. "It is a milder culture, not as sour as the cultures in the U.S. or Middle Eastern countries," Benoît says. "We use the lowest legal level of pasteurization, and a lot of lactose-intolerant people can actually digest this."

But the difference between Benoît's yogurt and everything else on the market is that his yogurt comes in returnable ceramic jars—just the way good yogurt is sold in France. "I started this from an idea in France," Benoît says.

That means that customers return the ceramic jars for a deposit, and not only is that environmentally friendly, but it makes it stand out even more. "Part of the thing is people who live in California have an easier time eating only local foods," Benoît says.

Besides using local milk, Benoît also uses local jam, fruit, and honey for his flavored versions, and his flavors have a much milder, less sugary taste than many other yogurts. "The sweet honey is just a little bit of heaven," Benoît says. "You can taste the *terroir* in it."

Because his yogurt is more fragile than varieties made with stabilizers, Benoît only sells his yogurt in California, at four farmers' markets and about 75 different stores. Many people who live across the United States have approached him about expanding his operations, but shipping the product via distributors would not maintain the integrity of his yogurt. Instead, Benoît says he would be interested in teaming up with other like-minded people across the country. "My vision is smaller. I'd like to replicate what is done here, but at small, organic dairies elsewhere," Benoît says. "Perhaps we would have a maple syrup yogurt on the East Coast. Rather than distribute my yogurt, I would rather conserve *terroir*. I want to keep this philosophy and work with *terroir*."

In the meantime, though, he's expanding his operations just a little bit in California, to keep up with the local demand, and his new dairy will accept visitors. "People taste my yogurt, and they like it," Benoît says. "I find people are very loyal. At some farmers' markets, I have customers who don't miss a Saturday."

STRAUS FAMILY CREAMERY

5600 Marshall Petaluma Road

Marshall, CA 94940

415-663-5464

www.strausfamilycreamery.com

ORGANIC COW'S MILK, BUTTER, YOGURT, AND ICE CREAM

Albert by the fence at his organic dairy, the first organic dairy and creamery in California.

Straus Family Creamery got its start when Bill Straus started farming with just 23 cows in Tomales Bay. The creamery started on its environmental path when Bill's wife, Ellen, read Rachel Carson's book *Silent Spring.* The family hasn't used herbicides and pesticides since the 1970s, and they haven't used fertilizers since the 1980s. Their son, Albert, grew up feeding calves and working around the farm, and when he went to Cal Poly, he majored in dairy husbandry and took a lot of classes in dairy manufacturing.

"I did my senior thesis on setting up a processing plant, but when I graduated, I came back to the farm and became partners with my father," Albert says. In 1990, someone approached him about producing organic milk for ice cream. "They gave up on the idea, but I kept looking into it," Albert says.

After spending more than three years of researching and then implementing the practices, Albert put together a business plan, and then on February 7, 1994, Straus Family Creamery became the first certified organic dairy and creamery west of the Mississippi River. Straus's glass bottles were a hit nationally, and this little dairy just north of San Francisco got a good buzz going about their practices and their products. "When we first came out, it was just four days after the federal government approved bovine growth hormone, and our label said we didn't have it," Albert says. "Then, we were told we couldn't put that on our label. It was a strange time."

They started with the milk, and then later added butter and cheese, and in 2003 they added ice cream. "When I was in college, I won third place in regional dairy products in ice cream, and that was the start of my weakness for ice cream," Albert says. "The message we relay about sustainable practices and farming comes through in our products, as they are high quality, with no additives, and they are minimally processed."

Their milk and milk products both have won awards and recognition, and their milk has also gained prominence because all of Cowgirl Creamery's cheeses are made with it. The family dairy has 300 cows, which are pastured on about 660 acres; they also purchase milk from two local, family farms, Hughes Dairy and Tresch Dairy. "The Tresch's became the second certified organic dairy in the state," Albert says. "Since 1996, they've been with me. I helped them transition."

The Strauss family farm boasts beautiful natural vistas.

The Strauses have also helped other family farms. Ellen founded the Marin County Agricultural Land Trust, which has preserved more than 40,000 acres in the last three decades. "I think that what we've been successful in, as an industry, is to keep small farms viable where the pressures have been to get bigger and bigger, and in California, to have five thousand or ten thousand cows on forty or sixty acres, in my mind, is not sustainable," Albert says. "Economic pressures have forced farmers to get that big, but then we have runoff issues and air quality issues. Small farms have the ability to be more sustainable, and it's something that can be passed on from generation to generation."

To become more sustainable, the Straus Family Creamery recently instituted a methane digester, which produces 90 percent of the electricity on the farm. "It captures methane, which is twenty times more detrimental as a greenhouse gas than carbon dioxide," Albert says. "It reduces odors on the farm, and I've seen an overall beneficial effect. I'm actually just putting together a fully electric truck. We try to stay ahead of the curve."

CHAPTER 7

The Artisan and Specialty COW'S MILK CHEESES

ANDANTE DAIRY

PICOLO

Delicate and sweet, this bloomy rind cheese is 100 percent-made from the milk of Jersey cows (from Larry Peter's herd at Spring Hill, actually). Made from milk and crème fraîche, this triple crème boasts a melt-on-your-tongue sweetness, with a touch of nuttiness.

ANDANTE DAIRY

PIANOFORTE

Modeled after St. Marcellin, this French-style bloomy rind has a soft, runny texture but a bold flavor. Since *pianoforte* means "soft and loud," this cheese offers the same combination, getting softer and creamier as it ages and increasing in flavor, too.

BELFIORE CHEESE COMPANY

FRESH AND SMOKED MOZZARELLA

This is a good snacking cheese with a smooth and gentle taste. The natural goodness of the milk comes through, and it has a clean taste. The smoked mozzarella is

stronger, and its aroma fills your mouth with its smoky goodness. It is smooth and savory, and it doesn't have any aftertaste. It would make a perfect addition to a barbecue chicken pizza or sandwich.

BELFIORE CHEESE COMPANY

FETA

This cow's milk feta is crumbly and good, with a slightly salty and tangy flavor. It is milder than some fetas on the market, and it would be a great addition to salads and wraps.

BELFIORE CHEESE COMPANY

FARMER'S CHEESE AND PANEER

Demand at local ethnic markets led cheese-maker Farr Hariri to develop first a farmer's cheese and then a paneer. The farmer's cheese is slighty tart and milky; it is made in the eastern European style, and it would make a good cheesecake or pastry filling.

The paneer is soft and gentle with a very, very mild flavor, which makes it the perfect complement to spicy Indian ingredients.

BELLWETHER FARMS
CARMODY

This award-winning cheese boasts a lovely golden color, which is derived from luscious Jersey milk, and it has a firm, semisoft texture. On your tongue it tastes buttery and rich, and it's easy to see how it earned best in its category in the London World Cheese Awards.

BELLWETHER FARMS
CRESCENZA

This traditional, square-shaped Italian cheese has no rind. Rich and decadent, it boasts some yeasty and tart notes, and it is one of the most buttery, unctuous cheeses on the planet. It's perfect for scooping up and spreading on baguettes, but it's equally good for use in cooking. It's really one of the most addictive cheeses around.

BRAVO FARMS HANDMADE CHEESE
SILVER MOUNTAIN

This is a bandage-wrapped, raw milk cheese that's rubbed in olive oil, and it is aged for at least nine months. Strong in flavor, it has an almost cheddar and Manchego blend of taste. It is a big, bold cheese with a lot of flavor.

BRAVO FARMS HANDMADE CHEESE
TULARE CANNONBALL

Shaped like, well, a cannonball, this is a Dutch Edam-style cheese, and it is aged for up to seven months. It is made with a 500-year-old recipe, and it has a bold, spicy flavor with a lot of depth.

BRAVO FARMS HANDMADE CHEESE

RACLETTE

This is one of the only American-made raclettes, and it just made its debut in late 2006. It is a great, Swiss-style cheese, and it's perfect for melting, especially in a raclette machine.

BRAVO FARMS HANDMADE CHEESE

WESTERN SAGE AND CHIPOTLE CHEDDARS

Though not as punched up as their bigger cheeses, Bravo Farms makes some really good cheddars. Their chipotle cheddar, which is made from raw milk, is spicy and hot, but not too overwhelming. Western Sage offers a lovely marbling of herbs, and it has won at the World Cheese Awards in London.

COWGIRL CREAMERY

RED HAWK

Bursting with taste, this washed rind, triple crème cheese is an American original

cheese. Made with organic milk from the Straus Creamery, this cheese has a red-hued rind and a creamy center. It offers layers of robust and pungent flavor, and it's no wonder that the American Cheese Society awarded it the coveted Best in Show in 2003.

COWGIRL CREAMERY

MT. TAM

Named for Mt. Tamalpais, which rises north of San Francisco, this organic cheese, made with milk from Straus Creamery, is a triple crème cheese that offers a buttery yet earthy flavor with notes of mushrooms. It won first place in the soft-ripened category in the 2008 American Cheese Society (ACS) competition.

COWGIRL CREAMERY

ST. PAT

Made to usher in springtime in Marin County, this cheese is wrapped with stinging nettle leaves. The nettles are first washed and frozen to make them stingless before they're applied to the cheese. Mellow and soft, the cheese marries with the smoky flavor of the nettles.

Fagundes Old World Cheese

St. John and St. Jorge
Portuguese Cheeses

St. Jorge is a traditional, Portuguese-style cheese, modeled after the cheeses that John Fagundes's great-grandmother made on the

Azores Islands. Made from raw cow's milk, it is aged for about three years, and it offers complex flavors with the right amount of sharpness. St. John is similar to St. Jorge, but it is a milder, raw milk cheese that is rubbed with extra virgin olive oil to give it a nice, natural rind. It offers a tangy, mild flavor that has enough depth to make it interesting. Both cheeses have won awards, including first place in their category at the ACS competition.

Fagundes Old World Cheese

Hanford Jack, Plain and Flavored

It's pretty easy to see how it's been considered the best jack in America, taking top honors in its category at the American Cheese Society competition. Mild and easy, it's a delectable cheese. Besides flavored, it comes in the hot but not too hot Santa Fe, which has smoky chipotle peppers added; smoked, which is nicely smoky; and San Joaquin, which is both smoky and tangy and highly flavorful. San Joaquin is my personal favorite.

FAGUNDES OLD WORLD CHEESE

HANFORD CHEDDAR

Golden-hued from Jersey milk, this mild cheddar is a gentle cheese, but it boasts a depth of flavor that most mild cheddars do not possess. It's a great snacking cheese, but it's also good for sandwiches, macaroni and cheese, and anything that calls for cheddar. It also comes smoked and in other flavors, too.

FISCALINI FARMSTEAD CHEESE COMPANY

BANDAGE-WRAPPED CHEDDAR

Aged between 18 and 30 months, this is real cheddar, the way cheddar was first made in England. Bolder in flavor than most cheddars in the United States, this is the real deal. Made from raw milk and bound in cloth, this cheese has a hard texture and a sharp taste with nutty undertones and an underlying sweetness. Cheesemaker Mariano Gonzalez's beauty became the first non-British cheese to win the Wyke Farms trophy for the Best Extra Mature Traditional Cheese category at the 2007 World Cheese Awards

Cheese is cheddared at Fiscalini Farmstead Cheese Company.

in London. It also regularly takes home wins from the American Cheese Society competition. If bandage-wrapped cheddars are a bit too strong for your liking, try regular or flavored Fiscalini cheddars instead. Especially good are the wine-washed Purple Moon cheddar and the Scotch ale–washed Hopscotch cheddar, and if you like cheese spreads, their horseradish cheddar cheese spread is simply divine.

FISCALINI FARMSTEAD CHEESE COMPANY

SAN JOAQUIN GOLD

This American original cheese is made from raw milk, and it is aged 16 months. It boasts a sweet and buttery taste. It is similar to a fontina, but it has more salt and is firmer than fontina.

FISCALINI FARMSTEAD CHEESE COMPANY

LIONZA

Aged for six months, this raw milk cheese is fruity and sweet, and it has small, irregular eyes and a semisoft texture. A very munchable cheese, it's great for a snack, but it also melts wonderfully in a fondue.

GIOIA CHEESE COMPANY

BURRATA

If you like fresh mozzarella, then you'll adore *burrata*. This is the creamiest, most succulent fresh mozzarella variety around. The outer shell of the fresh mozzarella ball is thin, and inside it is stuffed with real cream

and bits of fresh mozzarella curd. This cheese is creamy, sweet, and oh-so-smooth. It's pretty darn easy to eat an entire 1-pound ball of it just by yourself. But it's also fun to share it, and it can be served plain, sprinkled with honey or sugar, or accompanied by fruit. My dear friend Barrie Lynn, the cheese impresario, recommends serving it with a little sugar, cocoa, and espresso powder for a decadent dessert.

LOLETA CHEESE COMPANY

REAL HUMBOLDT GOLD

Made to benefit the Humboldt Arts Council, this creamy gold cheese has layers of flavor, as well as a gorgeous golden hue. It gets its great flavor from the 100 percent Jersey milk and three separate cultures. It's a great cheese for both snacking and cooking.

Cream City Cheddar benefits the Ferndale Museum.

LOLETA CHEESE COMPANY

GARDEN CHEDDAR

This is one of the many fine cheddars and jacks that Loleta Cheese makes. What I like best is its sweet, nutty flavor, making it the perfect cheese for that grilled cheese sandwich. As an added bonus, it benefits the Humboldt Botanical Gardens Foundation. Other good cheddars include the smoked salmon cheddar and the organic cheddar, too.

LOLETA CHEESE COMPANY

FONTINA

Buttery, with a depth of flavor and just a touch of tangy sweetness, this is a great melting cheese. Made from 100 percent Jersey milk, this is a great fontina to add to pizzas, pastas, and even grilled cheese, and it's easy to see why Wolfgang Puck likes to add this to his pizzas.

Humboldt Garden Cheddar supports the Humboldt Botanical Gardens Foundation.

LOLETA CHEESE COMPANY

HAVARTI

One of Loleta's specialty cheeses, the Havarti has small holes and a nice body. It has a sweet, balanced taste. Also made from 100 percent Jersey milk, it comes in a variety of flavors, the best of which is herb and spice. It has a great blend of onion, sweet pepper, and dill, and it is my sister Karen's favorite Havarti. She likes to add it to her spring risotto.

MARIN FRENCH CHEESE CO.

Schloss and Schlosskranz cheeses age at Marin French.

MARIN FRENCH CHEESE CO.

ROUGE ET NOIR LE PETITE CRÈME OR MARIN FRENCH GOLD

This decadent triple crème cheese is everything a triple crème should be—rich, soft, and creamy with a melt-in-your-mouth taste and texture. Soft-ripened and sweet, and made with milk that has no rBST added, it's an addictive cheese, and it's easy to see how it took Best American Cheese in the 2007 World Cheese Awards. And it was declared world's best Brie in the 2005 World Cheese Awards, becoming the first non-French Brie to win in that category in the history of the competition. It also won the Best Soft-Ripened Cheese category in the 2003 American Cheese Society (ACS) competition.

MARIN FRENCH CHEESE CO.

YELLOW BUCK CAMEMBERT OR LE PETIT CAMEMBERT

Decadent and luscious, this soft-ripened cheese has a fuller taste than a Brie does. More expansive in taste, with an inherent nuttiness, it is quite delicious. Like the triple crème, it's an award winner, taking home the 2005 Best American Cheese trophy at the World Cheese Awards in London.

MARIN FRENCH CHEESE CO.

SCHLOSS AND SCHLOSSKRANZ

This Austrian-style cheese, similar to Liederkranz, is a smear-ripened, washed rind cheese. Schloss, which means "castle," has a robust flavor, and it is aged up to five months. It has a tawny hue, and it fills your mouth with flavor. Not a cheese for the fainthearted, but it is a cheese for those who love great, strong cheeses.

MARIN FRENCH CHEESE CO.

ROUGE ET NOIR MARIN FRENCH BLUE AND LE PETITE BLEU

Similar to the German, soft-ripened Cambozola, this is a soft-ripened, bloomy rind cheese that has delicate veins of blue running through it. It sort of tastes like a cross between Brie and Roquefort, and it's quite delightful.

Mini wheels of Brie age at Marin French.

MID-COAST CHEESE COMPANY/FRANKLIN'S TELEME

TELEME

This natural-rind, semisoft cheese is dusted with rice powder on the outside. Luscious, melt-in-your-mouth delicious, this is a California original cheese. Tangy, with an almost lemony tinge, this cheese is great for both eating and cooking. It is wonderful to add to pizzas, pastas, and sauces, but it is equally good by itself or just accompanied by fresh fruit.

peppers. Perfect for snacking, but even better on grilled cheese sandwiches or on burgers.

SPRING HILL JERSEY CHEESE

DRY JACK

This award-winning cheese is a little salty, but moist, and it has a nice sharp tang to it and a lovely, chocolate-colored rind. It's a good munching cheese, and it's won national accolades for its delicious taste.

SPRING HILL JERSEY CHEESE

BREEZE

This mild, Brie-like cheese has a soft-ripened, bloomy rind, and a very mild, buttery taste. Made from the milk of an organic, all-Jersey cow herd, it is delicate and delicious.

THREE SISTERS FARMSTEAD CHEESE

SERENA

This American original cheese is aged up to a year. Firm and smooth, it has rich and nutty flavor with definite nuances. Made from raw Jersey milk, the cheese has a rind that is rubbed with oil and vinegar during the curing process. Quite delicious, it's easy to see why it's won numerous awards from the American Cheese Society.

SPRING HILL JERSEY CHEESE

WHITE CHEDDAR

Aged from one to two years, this raw-milk, organic cheddar is firm, rich, and buttery, and it's my friend Damon's favorite cheddar. It also comes in flavors of garlic, sage, and

THREE SISTERS FARMSTEAD CHEESE

SERENITA

Another ACS award winner also made with raw Jersey milk, Serenita was first crafted in error, but make no mistake about it, this is a great cheese. Sweet and buttery, this is an easy cheese to eat, and it just gets better with each bite.

VELLA CHEESE COMPANY

MONTEREY JACK

Plenty of cheesemakers in California make a good jack cheese, but Ig Vella and his cheese-maker Charles Malkassian make some of the best jack in the world. Mild and delicious, this jack is crafted by hand, in small batches, just the way Ig's father made it.

VELLA CHEESE COMPANY

DRY JACK

While Ig's regular Monterey Jack is wonderful, his Dry Jack is even better. Aged for up to two years, this cheese is coated with oil, cocoa powder, and pepper, and since the

cheeses are rolled by hand and shaped in a muslin cloth, each cheese has an imprint of the cloth on the back, an attribute that no factory-made cheese ever has. It has a nice bite, and a hard, crumbly texture. It's great for eating, but it is also wonderful for grating, too. And while some cheesemakers make both a regular and Dry Jack, Ig also makes a Mezzo Seco, a cheese that isn't as dry as Dry Jack, nor as perishable as regular jack. It was originally invented as a summer cheese when refrigeration wasn't as widespread, but then fell out of favor. Ig revived it in 1999. The Dry Jack was the U.S. Cheese Champion cheese in 1995–96, while the regular Jack has earned numerous awards in several competitions.

VELLA CHEESE COMPANY

ROMANELLO

Similar to Romano cheese, this Italian-inspired cheese was last made in 1992 until Ig decided to make it

again recently. It is a cow's milk version of Romano, and it is a good grating cheese. Also, it took second place at the American Cheese Society in its category in 2005.

VELLA CHEESE COMPANY
TOMA

Another Italian-inspired cheese, the Toma is a creamy, semisoft cheese that was originally made in the Piedmont area of Italy. It has won numerous first and second place medals in several cheese competitions, including the American Cheese Society's annual awards.

WINCHESTER CHEESE COMPANY
AGED AND FLAVORED GOUDAS

For real Dutch Gouda, it doesn't get any more authentic than Winchester. This wonderful little cheese company makes some stellar Goudas that win regularly at the annual American Cheese Society competition. The Goudas range, in order of youngest to oldest: the mild, aged two months; the medium, aged three to four months; the sharp, aged six to eight months; and the super, aged a year and up. The mild and medium Goudas offer a great milk flavor. But the sharp and the super aged are the best of the bunch, as they boast firm, drier textures and a more caramel-like color. As Gouda ages, its texture has more of a Parmesan-like feel to it than the semisoft firmness you'd expect in a Gouda. They are quite delightful cheeses, and it's easy to see how the sharp took a bronze at the 2004 World Cheese Awards in London. Try the garden herb, smoked, jalapeño, or cumin flavors.

CHAPTER 8

The Artisan and Specialty GOAT'S AND SHEEP'S MILK CHEESES

ANDANTE DAIRY

IMPROMPTU

Whenever cheesemaker Soyoung Scanlan has a surplus of milk, she makes this aged, hard, goat's milk or mixed milk cheese. Similar to a pecorino in style, it offers sweet and nutty notes and a touch of butterscotch.

ANDANTE DAIRY

TRIO

This is a bloomy rind, mixed milk cheese of both cow's milk and goat's milk, as well as crème fraiche. It has the tartness you'd expect from a goat's milk cheese, but it has more of the mushroomy flavor of a Camembert. When it is young, you can taste the goat's milk flavors more strongly, but as it ages, it takes on more of the cow's milk flavors.

BELLWETHER FARMS

SAN ANDREAS

This raw sheep's milk cheese is aged up to three months, and it's an American original. It has a nice, nutty flavor, and it's won several awards. It's no wonder it received top honors in its category at the World Cheese Awards in London.

BELLWETHER FARMS

PEPATO

Another raw, sheep's milk cheese, this semi-soft cheese is aged up to three months, but what makes it stand out are the whole peppercorns that stud the entire wheel, giving a piquant accent to the creamy cheese.

BUBALUS BUBALIS

MOZZARELLA DI BUFALA

If you've never tasted mozzarella *di bufala,* then you've been missing out. This authentic mozzarella is made with the milk of water buffalo. Fresh, clean, and milky, it has a depth of flavor, and it's different than most fresh mozzarellas, which are made with cow's milk. Best eaten fresh, it will get softer and more intense in flavor the longer you leave it in its water container. When you cut into a juicy ball, liquid oozes out of it. It tastes amazing in a Capri salad, but it can also be used in pastas and pizzas, too.

BUBALUS BUBALIS
RICOTTA

Made from the whey leftover from moz-zarella *di bufala* production, this ricotta is sweet, rich, and creamy, and like the moz-zarella, it is made with water buffalo's milk. It has a richer and sweeter taste than most other ricottas, and it would be delightful in pasta and pastry applications.

CYPRESS GROVE CHÈVRE
HUMBOLDT FOG

The first time I tasted Humboldt Fog, I had just returned from a trip to the Loire Valley; I had been looking all over for this, rare not usually imported French aged goat's milk cheese. One bite of Humboldt Fog, and I nearly swooned—this was exactly the kind of cheese I was looking for. Though Hum-

boldt Fog is an American original cheese, its roots are decidedly French. A bloomy rind cheese, it is coated with ash, with a line of ash down the middle. It is a complex cheese with layers of tang, and it becomes creamier with age. It's won numerous awards, including being mentioned as one of the top 100 designs by *Metropolitan Home* magazine in 2003.

CYPRESS GROVE CHÈVRE

Humboldt Fog is immediately recognizable by the dark line of ash in the middle of the cheese.

CYPRESS GROVE CHÈVRE
PURPLE HAZE

This is Cypress Grove's most popular fresh chèvre, and it's easy to see why. Lavender and fennel pollen are a delightful sweet accent to the tangy, fresh chèvre. It also has won numerous awards, including several firsts in assorted competitions.

CYPRESS GROVE CHÈVRE
TRUFFLE TREMOR

As the newest in Cypress Grove's lineup, this cheese delivers a big wallop of truffle flavor. This bloomy rind cheese is buttery yet earthy and aromatic, and it contains bits of real truffle in every bite. It's an utterly decadent cheese.

CYPRESS GROVE CHÈVRE
BERMUDA TRIANGLE

This triangle-shaped bloomy rind cheese has an unusual advantage because of its structure (it looks like a triangle log); it is easily sliced into delicate little triangles for cheese plates. It offers a mild, earthy flavor, and its creami-ness increases as it ages. It has received several firsts, including three at the American Cheese Society competitions.

DÉLICE DE LA VALLÉE/
THE EPICUREAN CONNECTION
DELICE DE LA VALLEE TRIPLE CRÈME
GOAT'S MILK AND COW'S MILK BLEND

Oh-so-creamy and smooth, this delightful cheese can be used in both savory and sweet dishes. Made from a blend of cow's milk and

Cypress Grove Chèvre's factory.

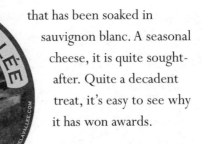

goat's milk, this triple crème has a light taste, but it is really rich. It is sort of like a cross between a chèvre and a *fromage blanc*. Cheesemaker and caterer Sheana Davis uses it with golden raspberries and honey, but she will also add herbs and nuts, too. It's also just wonderful with no additions at all, and it's quite addictive.

FAGUNDES OLD WORLD CHEESE

GOAT'S MILK CHEDDAR AND JACK

This chalk-white cheddar offers a mild flavor with just a slight tanginess. The jack is creamy, again with just a little tang of goat's milk flavor. Both are delicious, aged goat's milk cheeses.

GOAT'S LEAP CHEESE

KIKU

Aged for up to four weeks, this wonderful goat's milk cheese is wrapped in a fig leaf that has been soaked in sauvignon blanc. A seasonal cheese, it is quite sought-after. Quite a decadent treat, it's easy to see why it has won awards.

GOAT'S LEAP CHEESE

CARMELA

This raw milk goat's milk cheese is aged for at least four months, but it tastes best at a year, when its flavors are at their peak. Its rind is dusted with paprika, and it has a firm texture and good depth of flavor.

HARLEY FARMS GOAT DAIRY

FLAVORED FRESH CHÈVRES

Light and creamy, these beauties might be the prettiest fresh chèvres on the planet, as each round or log is decorated with edible flowers, dried fruits, or nuts. The Van Goat not only has beautiful flowers on the outside, but hidden in the middle are some fresh lavender blossoms, which adds just a touch of sweetness. The Apricot Pistachio smelled nutty and perfect, with the apricot's tartness balanced by the cheese's mellow nature. My friend Stephen, who was tasting the cheeses with me, simply said "It's dessert." Cranberry Walnut is sweeter and not so tart, while the Tomato Basil is sweet and tangy. The Garlic Herb was almost fluffy with chives, tangy and rich. Stephen, who loves garlic-flavored fresh cheeses, described it as "a thousand times better than Boursin spread."

HARLEY FARMS GOAT DAIRY
RICOTTA

This ricotta is very creamy with a clean, milky taste. Light on the palate, it has no aftertaste, and it is fresher than most ricottas. It's easy to see why a local ravioli company uses this by the gallon. It makes a great pasta filler.

LAURA CHENEL
FRESH CHÈVRE

One of the most renowned chèvres in the country, Laura Chenel's Chèvre is tangy and sweet, and it comes in a variety of sizes, shapes, and flavors. The Chabis is a fresh, spreadable cheese that comes in dill, black pepper, or herbs. It is delicate and sweetly tangy. The Log comes in the traditional French log shape, and it is probably the Laura Chenel cheese that most people are most familiar with. It has the right amount of tang, and it is perfect for slicing, rolling in

Goats graze on rich California pastures.

bread crumbs, and then broiling before topping a salad.

LAURA CHENEL
TAUPINIÈRE

The Taupinière is a slightly aged goat cheese with a bloomy rind and outer layer of ash. It has a depth of flavor that made my cousin Kyle swoon after she tasted it. It not only tastes good, but its mound shape makes it a beautiful addition to any cheese plate.

LAURA CHENEL
CABECOU

Cabecou are slightly aged rounds of goat cheese marinated in olive oil. They are more dense in texture than traditional chèvre, and they have a nuttier, more intense flavor.

LAURA CHENEL
TOMME

Weighing between 3 and 4 pounds per wheel, this cheese is aged for six months. It offers a firmer texture and a mellow yet rich taste.

MARIN FRENCH CHEESE CO.
ROUGE ET NOIR LE PETITE CHÈVRE AND MARIN FRENCH CHÈVRE

This is Marin County French's goat's milk version of Brie, in either the small, 4-ounce size or the large 24-ounce size. Soft-ripened and creamy, this is a tangy and sweet Brie.

MARIN FRENCH CHEESE CO.
ROUGE ET NOIR LE PETITE CHÈVRE BLEU AND MARIN FRENCH CHÈVRE BLEU

This is similar to a German Cambazola cheese—a cheese that tastes like a combination of Brie and blue cheese. But this is Marin County French's goat's milk version, and it tastes quite lovely with delicate, little blue veins running through the soft cheese.

Pug's Leap Farm

Pavé

Pavé is a lush and gentle, sweet bloomy rind cheese that is aged from three to four weeks. It comes in a truncated pyramid shape, and it has a bit of an earthy or mushroomy flavor. Cheesemaker Pascal Destandau says it peaks at a month and gets a bit stronger. It's truly a memorable cheese.

Pug's Leap Farm

Bûche

The Bûche is aged from three to four weeks; it comes in a log shape. Smooth and tangy, it has a drier texture than Destandau's other cheeses.

Pug's Leap Farm

Petit Marceau and Grand Marceau

Aged only two weeks, the Petit Marceau comes in smaller rounds while the Grand Marceau comes in, not surprisingly, larger rounds. Both are lovely, tart cheeses, and the Grand Marceau's subtle flavor lingers a bit longer in your mouth after you've indulged in it.

Pug's Leap Farm

Macas

The newest cheese to Destandau's lineup, this delicious cheese is named for the terms of endearment that Destandau and his partner Eric Smith's intern, Lali Rodriguez, call the goats. Tart and sweet, it is a yummy cheese.

Redwood Hill Farm and Creamery

Chèvre

Jennifer Bice makes great chèvre, sweet, tangy, and creamy, and it comes in the most darling little containers. It also comes in plain, garlic-chive, or three-peppercorn varieties. My favorite is the three-peppercorn, which has just enough bite. It has won many awards.

REDWOOD HILL FARM AND CREAMERY

GRAVENSTEIN GOLD

This is simply a fabulous washed rind cheese. Golden hued on the outside and creamy on the inside, this cheese gets its color from hard cider made in nearby orchards (of Gravenstein apples, of course). It boasts a great depth of flavor, and its taste changes as it ages. This is a cheese to watch.

REDWOOD HILL FARM AND CREAMERY

BUCHERET

This soft-ripened, bloomy rind is aged between two to four weeks. It has a nice, sharp tang to it that gets stronger as it ages. This cheese has won several awards.

REDWOOD HILL FARM AND CREAMERY

CAMELLIA

This soft-ripened, bloomy rind is aged from six to eight weeks, and it is somewhat like a goat's milk version of Camembert. It gets softer and creamier as it ages, offering a delicious taste from beginning to end, and it is no wonder that it has received numerous awards.

RINCONADA DAIRY

POZO TOMME

Nutty and fruity, with layers and layers of flavor, this is a great aged sheep's milk cheese. Made of raw milk and aged from two months on up, this cheese gets harder and more complex as it ages. It could be comparable to some of the great pecorinos of Italy, as it is also a wonderful grating cheese. In 2007, The Cheese Store of Beverly Hills awarded it first place among the aged sheep's milk cheese in its American Artisanal Treasures competition.

RINCONADA DAIRY
LA PANZA GOLD
Washed with whey, this lovely aged raw milk sheep's cheese has a gorgeous golden hue to it, and an equally lovely taste. Earthy yet fruity, this complex cheese won first place in its category at the 2005 American Cheese Society competition.

RINCONADA DAIRY
CHAPARRAL
One of the only mixed milk cheeses crafted in California, this is a blend of two thirds sheep's milk and one third goat's milk. Aged for at least two months, it has a natural rind.

Smooth and creamy, the rich nuances of its flavor come from whatever the goats and sheep eat on the pasture the day they are milked.

SOLEDAD GOATS
FRESH CHÈVRE
Light and tangy, this fresh chèvre is quite delightful. But what makes it even more delicious are all the inventive flavors that cheesemaker Carol Pierce comes up with. Cilantro and spring onion, salmon and dill, garlic and herb . . . the list is practically endless, as Carol uses 14 different herbs and spices for her creative concoctions. But perhaps one of her best is her lavender and lemon, which took a gold medal at the 2005 World Cheese Awards in London. It also received the Perpetual Cup from the Frome Cheese Show in England. Besides fresh chèvre, Carol also makes delicious chèvre buttons, which she preserves in extra virgin olive oil and herbs.

CHAPTER 9

The Specialty and Artisan
HISPANIC
CHEESES

California makes more Hispanic- or Latino-style cheeses than any other state. In fact, California makes two thirds of all Hispanic-style cheeses crafted in the United States—a whopping 100 million-plus pounds every year, double what it was in 1997. "We make more Hispanic cheese than any other state," says Lynne Devereux, president of the California Artisan Cheese Guild.

The state makes 25 distinct Hispanic-style cheeses. The cheeses tend to fall in one of two categories: fresh or aged. Fresh Hispanic cheeses are made to be sold fresh, in the same way chèvre or fresh mozzarella is made to be sold fresh. But aged Hispanic cheeses aren't aged the way European cheeses are: They're aged for a period of weeks, not months.

A few varieties of Hispanic-style cheeses that are worth noting include:

QUESO FRESCO (KAY-so FRESS-ko), which literally means "fresh cheese," is a white cheese, sometimes made with cow's and goat's milks combined, and is similar to a farmer's cheese. It is crumbly and tangy, and when heated, it will soften, but not melt.

QUESO PANELA (KAY-so PAHN-ay-la) is sometimes known as *queso de canasta* or "basket cheese" because it often has an imprint of a basket on it. This fresh cheese, in addition to being added to dishes, sometimes is cut up into pieces and fried— straight, as an appetizer by itself—because it will retain its shape when cooked.

QUESO BLANCO (Kay-so BLAN-ko) or "white cheese" is the most popular cheese in Mexico and Latin America. It is a fresh cheese typically made from skimmed milk, and it is much like a cross between cottage cheese and mozzarella.

QUESO OAXACA (KAY-so wha-HA-ka) is a melting cheese, and it is often used to fill quesadillas. It originated, naturally, in the Oaxaca region of Mexico.

QUESO COTIJA (KAY-so KO-tee-ha) is a firm, salty cheese, and it is one of the aged Hispanic cheeses. It is similar to a dry feta and is often used in soups, salads, and bean dishes.

QUESO ASADERO (KAY-so AH-sah-DAY-ro), which means "aged cheese," is a melting cheese that is rather like provolone in taste. It is often used to make a Mexican fondue.

There are at least 15 cheesemakers who craft these traditional cheeses, but there are less than a handful of these cheesemakers who run artisan cheesemaking operations. Two who do are Fagundes Old World Farmstead Cheese in Hanford, and Loleta Cheese Company in Loleta. In fact, both could be considered farmstead cheesemakers, as Fagundes's John Fagundes is a multi-generational dairyman, as is Loleta's Bob Laffranchi. Whereas John went into cheesemaking after being a dairyman, Bob got into it after being an agricultural teacher at a local high school. Both, however, got into making Hispanic-style cheeses because of the growing market demand.

Hispanic cheese is a growing area in the market, says John. "Within ten years the majority of California's population will be Hispanic, and this is a very big opportunity for sales," John says. His line of Hispanic cheeses is called Maria's Queso, named after his Portuguese grandmother who made cheese.

Bob got into the making of the cheese as a special, one-time request. "A grocer actually approached us and asked us if we could make this cheese because he didn't have a source with consistent quality," Bob says. "To make this cheese, he brought up his father, who could not speak English, to teach us how to make the cheese. The cheese has been a hit."

Bob says he has plans to make other Hispanic-style cheeses, but he and his team of cheesemakers are working to develop the exact recipe that they will be satisfied with. "We're developing make procedures from Mexico," Bob says. "I know there's some market potential there."

What also should be noted is that another strength California has in making these cheeses comes from the diversity of the cheesemakers themselves. While not all cheesemakers who craft Hispanic cheeses are of Latino descent, some are, and there are many Latino cheesemakers who should be rising up through the ranks at creameries throughout the state in the upcoming years, and it will be exciting to see how they impact cheese.

FAGUNDES OLD WORLD FARMSTEAD CHEESE

MARIA'S COTIJA

Fagundes makes three really nice Hispanic-style cheeses. The boldest of the three is Maria's *Cotija*, which is an aged Hispanic cheese. It is sharp, definitively tangy, and it has an almost cheddar-esque flavor, except it is much stronger and more biting than a typical cheddar, plus it is much more grainy and crumbly than even some 10-year-old aged cheddars. It is a white cheese with a dusty orange rind, and it crumbles readily. Not only good for Mexican and

Latin American dishes, this cheese also is a good substitute for Parmesan-type cheeses, and it tastes great in Caesar salads. And since Caesar salads were actually invented in Mexico, it's a fitting substitute. It is made with rBST-free milk too.

FAGUNDES OLD WORLD FARMSTEAD CHEESE
MARIA'S QUESO PANELA

Queso Panela is milky, creamy, and crumbly, and unlike most similar-style *quesos,* it is made with whole milk, not skim. It is also made from the milk of one, single farmstead herd, and it is rBST-free. It is also quite tangy and very salty, with the taste of fresh, clean milk. It's so fresh and moist that it is also squeaky, almost in the same way fresh cheese curds are squeaky.

FAGUNDES OLD WORLD FARMSTEAD CHEESE
MARIA'S QUESO FRESCO

Queso Fresco is very similar to *Queso Panela,* but it is a bit softer in texture. Like *Queso*

Panela, it has a very milky yet slightly tart taste. It's quite delicious. "It is a very mild cheese, with no culture added to it," John says. "It really has a fresh taste."

FAGUNDES OLD WORLD FARMSTEAD CHEESE
PORTUGUESE QUEIJO FRESCO

Portuguese *Queijo Fresco* is also very similar to these two cheeses in both taste and texture, but the main difference is it is made only with whole milk from the morning milking of the herd.

LOLETA CHEESE
QUESO FRESCO

Fresh, with just a slight tang, this is a very milky, soft cheese, and the pasture grazing of the cows comes through in the clean taste. Also, it is rBST-free. Unlike most of Loleta's cheeses, which are made with the milk of Jersey cows, this cheese is made with the

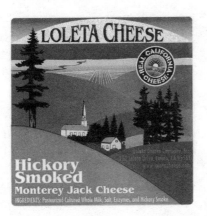

milk of Holsteins, because Jersey milk has a more yellowish tinge to it due to the higher carotene content in the milk. "In Hispanic cheeses, yellow is not a good thing," Bob says. So he uses milk from a separate herd of Holsteins to make sure that the milk has a purer white color.

CHAPTER 10

Other Artisan
DAIRY
PRODUCTS

BELLWETHER FARMS
SHEEP'S MILK YOGURT

Rich and creamy, sheep's milk yogurt fills your mouth and coats your tongue more than a typical cow's milk yogurt. It boasts a lovely, sweet taste, and comes in a variety of flavors, including blueberry, blackberry, and vanilla.

HUMBOLDT CREAMERY
ORGANIC ICE CREAM

The sweet cream of the organic Jersey milk comes through in the ice cream, making this rich treat one to savor. Though the creamery makes dozens of different flavors of ice cream, their organic line is their best. For purists, try their vanilla, a sweet and clean milky taste, perfect for shakes and sundaes.

Strawberry—and other fruit flavors—has actual strawberries in the cream and no artificial colors. The chocolate has a real, dark cocoa and very chocolaty flavor. But my favorite, hands down, is espresso chip—a rich coffee base with dark chocolate bits swirled in. Any which flavor you try, it's addictive.

KENDALL CHEESE COMPANY
CRÈME FRAÎCHE

Rich, creamy, and unctuous, this crème fraîche is a cook's dream, and it is no wonder that it has taken first place several times in its category at the American Cheese Society's annual competition. Tangy and sweet, with a clean flavor, it is perfect for topping fruits and desserts, but it also has a plethora of savory uses as well. It makes great cream sauces, and it is luscious when added to cream that is whipped, giving it a frothier, fuller foam. Cheesemaker Sadie Kendall recommends adding it in half-and-half proportions to whipping cream, and she also suggests mixing in herbs and letting it sit in the refrigerator before adding it to sauces, to give the sauces extra depth and fragrance. Frankly, it also tastes great just straight out of the carton!

ST. BENOÎT YOGURT

PLAIN, FLAVORED COW'S MILK YOGURTS

Rich and creamy, this yogurt is a yogurt lover's dream. With a fresh milk taste and a very subtle tang, it is, quite simply put, one of the best yogurts in the country, and it is the only yogurt in the United States that is sold in returnable ceramic jars. Made with whole milk from an all-Jersey herd, the yogurt has a smoother, thicker body, and it doesn't have any stabilizers or thickeners. It tastes great plain, but its honey and Meyer lemon versions are to die for. The honey has a gentle, clean sweetness, and the Meyer lemon is tangy without being overpowering. Also quite good are its fruit flavors, including strawberry, plum, and boysenberry. And what's more, less sugar is used in the process, and all the ingredients—the honey and the fruits—are local, too.

STRAUS FAMILY CREAMERY

ORGANIC MILK, CREAM

If you've never had non-homogenized, organic milk, then you're in for a treat. The milk is pasteurized at 170 degrees for 19 seconds, which is unlike the ultra-high temperature pasteurization that most milks undergo. The milk proteins aren't broken down by homogenization, and the cream in the milk rises to the top. The slower pasteurization and lack of homogenization keep the milk's natural flavors intact, and it's easy to taste them; the milk is sweet and clean. It's really one of the best milks around. The company also makes delicious butter and delectable ice cream, and all of its products are minimally processed, which means higher quality and more taste. Straus also makes great ice cream.

LALOO'S GOAT'S MILK ICE CREAM COMPANY

GOAT'S MILK ICE CREAM AND FROZEN YOGURT

Rich and creamy, you wouldn't know by tasting it that Laloo's ice cream is made from goat's milk instead of cow's milk. Though it has less than half the fat and calories of most premium ice creams, it doesn't sacrifice any of the taste. Vanilla Snowflake is a delicious vanilla ice cream, but what Laloo's does extraordinarily well is to come up with some incredibly innovative flavors. With more than a dozen to choose from, it's hard to narrow down a favorite. Try Cherries

Tuilerie, chock-full of cherry goodness; Strawberry Darling, filled with big bites of real strawberries and large, syrupy swaths of balsamic reduction; or Rumplemint, rich minty ice cream filled with lots of dark chocolate bits. It's no wonder it was recognized as a special selection by the Food Network 2007 Awards. Kosher and Free Farm Humane certified to boot.

REDWOOD HILL FARM AND CREAMERY

KEFIR AND YOGURT

Redwood Hill Farm and Creamery has been making great yogurt for more than two decades, but just this past year the company added the decidedly delicious kefir to the lineup. Kefir is sort of like drinkable yogurt, but it has different and more cultures—it has 10 different live and active cultures. Available in plain and blueberry-pomegranate (with açai) flavors, it is creamy and tastes like

CARRYON COMMUNICATIONS, INC., KRIS ELLENBERG

a yogurt smoothie. Especially delicious is the blueberry-pomegranate.

SPRING HILL JERSEY CHEESE
CULTURED BUTTER, PLAIN AND FLAVORED
Rich and creamy, this butter is great for slathering on morning toast or corn on the cob. Though I'm not much of a fan of flavored butters, I'm hooked on Spring Hill Jersey's Lemon Shallot Cultured butter. It tastes amazing on regular rolls, but I love using it in place of garlic on toasted Italian bread. Spring Hill also has a zesty garlic butter that's good, too.

CHAPTER 11

The Future of CALIFORNIA CHEESE

Just 15 short years ago, California edged out Wisconsin in overall milk production, and its dominance has yet to be topped by the "Dairy State" or any other state for that matter. Not only does California lead in fluid milk production, but it also makes more butter, yogurt, and ice cream than any other state. In less than 30 years, California went from making about 16 million pounds of cheese annually to exceeding 2.29 billion pounds a year. Nowhere in the United States has the dairy industry seen such phenomenal growth.

For the last five years, dairy experts have been predicting that the Golden State will edge "whey" ahead of Wisconsin in overall cheese production, and in California there's an almost tangible sense of excitement about this accomplishment, which will then make the state the fifth largest dairy-producing region in the world. California, it must be noted, already leads in mozzarella and Hispanic-style cheese production, and it's way ahead in

Workers package Marin French's cheese in the early 20th century.

Marin French's future, along with that of all California cheeses, looks bright.

terms of dairy exports to Asia and Latin America, too.

But while all this commodity-style growth is worth noting, it's not what I or other caseophiles find most intriguing. What's most inspiring is the still-growing artisan side of the dairy industry. The California Milk Advisory Board has assisted and inspired some traditional dairies to move into the artisan arena, and they've been a big champion of California artisan cow's milk cheeses, too. But perhaps the biggest evidence that California artisans have come of age, so to speak, is that in late 2005 the California Artisan Cheese Guild was founded.

Organized by dedicated cheesemakers across the state, the guild fills a necessary gap. Members are dedicated to promoting specialty cheesemakers and their incredible cow, goat, sheep, and even buffalo milk cheeses. The organization hosts trainings, seminars, and events, as well as provides a more informal support network for artisan cheesemakers. In a sense, it's sort of like a miniature American Cheese Society just for California cheesemakers.

Though the guild is new, its impact could be big. Another interesting sign of California's artisanal strength is a new magazine called *Culture* that is just starting up. Similar to a *Wine Enthusiast,* except that it is about cheese, this magazine was started by some California cheese lovers. It covers cheese issues across the country, but the fact that it is headquartered in California says something.

The magazine has a lot to write about. Almost every year these cheesemakers come up with new and exciting cheeses, and they're constantly pushing the envelope in terms of quality, flavor, and ingenuity. At the same time, many of them also are quite concerned with the environment, and they're aware that if California is going to continue to be a great agricultural state, then agricultural lands must be preserved. The Marin County Land Trust, the Sonoma County Land Trust, and other organizations like them are actively working to preserve the farmlands that make California's agricultural prowess possible.

Whey drains from the cheese at Harley Farms.

California also really is a leader in the movement of organic farming. Some dairymen, Albert Straus perhaps preeminent among them, are working for greater sustainability in farming. "All over the world, I think, farmers are kind of conservative in the sense that they want to see that something is working and feasible before they try something themselves," says Albert, who heads up Straus Family Creamery. "I think I've been able to demonstrate that organic is not only feasible, but that it's taken off. Indeed, on the North Coast of California,

143

The flowers that adorn Harley Farms' chèvre grow right outside the creamery's doors.

organic is the hope for farmers who want to stay in the dairy business."

When these pioneering cheesemakers and dairy folk first started, they didn't have resources like the California Cheese Guild or the American Cheese Society to help them. But what they did have is a nation of chefs who were hungry for their handcrafted products. Today, the market is more crowded than it was even 10 years ago, but there's always room for quality cheesemakers who carve out their own niche. Many California cheesemakers have garnered big followings for their small cheeses by selling them at farmers' markets throughout the state. I especially recommend the Ferry Plaza Market in San Francisco, but just about any local market has at least one local cheesemaker. And there's just something so satisfying about picking up your chèvre or your cheddar from the cheesemaker herself.

It's my desire, as I write this, that you fall for California cheese the way I have—with a head over heels, passionate adoration for its creamy, diverse goodness. And fortunately, for people like me who sometimes dream of very specific and tasty California cheeses, many of them are available in gourmet grocery stores and cheese counters across the country. Most, but not all, can also be shipped to you if you get a craving.

As I write this, I know of one internationally known cheesemaker who is relocating his creamery to California, and I've heard of a few other cheesemakers who'd like to come online. It truly is an exciting time for California cheese. But then again, if you're a foodie, California is always an exciting place to live or to visit. And especially if you love cheese, then California is definitely the place to be. In fact, if I wasn't married to a firmly rooted Midwestern boy, it wouldn't be that hard to pack my bags and head west. I'm told I have an open invitation.

CHAPTER 12

THE CHEESEMAKERS
Who Invite Visitors

Many of the cheesemakers and artisanal dairy folk in California not only accept visitors, but they delight in sharing their passion for cheese with fans. Some of them have formal stores where one can drop in any time to visit. Others do not have formal stores, but they do invite visitors by appointment if people call ahead of time, or they host annual events in which they open their doors. One, Rinconada Dairy, actually has a farmstead bed and breakfast where you can spend the night.

DROP-IN VISITS

BRAVO FARMS HANDMADE CHEESE

36005 Highway 99
Traver, CA 93673
559-897-4634
1-800-610-FARM
www.bravofarms.com

HOURS: 7 AM–7 PM, daily

DESCRIPTION: This fantastic little creamery also has a great café, a small garden with chickens out back, and a fun country store. They also have viewing windows to the creamery so you can see exactly how their award-winning cheddars and other cheeses are produced. It's also worth stopping for a bite to eat in their café, too.

COWGIRL CREAMERY

80 Fourth Street
Point Reyes Station, CA 94956
415-663-9335
www.cowgirlcreamery.com

HOURS: 10–6, Wednesday through Sunday

DESCRIPTION: Tiny, but mighty, this Marin County creamery not only has viewing windows and an amazing little store, but they also have a great selection of artisanal cheeses from around the globe. Their little deli counter/café also serves up some great soups, salads, and sandwiches.

FAGUNDES OLD WORLD CHEESE

8700 Fargo Avenue
Hanford, CA 93230
559-582-2000

ALSO

FARIA'S RANCH MARKET

8606 Avenue 280
Visalia, CA 93277
559-651-0994

HOURS: 8–4:30, Monday through Friday at the creamery; 10–6, Monday through Saturday at the market

DESCRIPTION: Driving to the creamery, you'll see fields and fields of what appear to be grape vines, but they're not grapes—they're kiwis. Besides making award-winning cow's milk and goat's milk cheeses, Fagundes also is a big producer of organic kiwis. So when the kiwis are in season, you can pick up some fruit to go along with your cheddar, Jack, Portuguese, or Hispanic cheeses!

FISCALINI CHEESE COMPANY

7296 Kernan Avenue
Modesto, CA 95358
209-545-5495
1-800-610-FARM
www.fiscalinicheese.com

HOURS: By the time this book is in your hands, Fiscalini's new cheese plant and retail store should be built, or almost completed. As of this writing, their little cheese operation has a retail cooler, which is open 7–4, Monday through Friday.

DESCRIPTION: This is out in the heart of cow country, and not only can you taste some great cheese here, but you can also visit with the cows and their baby calves, too. Though I haven't visited the new plant and store, the plans are gorgeous, indeed, and I can't wait to visit and taste more of master cheesemaker Mariano Gonzales's wonderful creations.

HARLEY FARMS GOAT DAIRY

205 North Street
Pescadero, CA 94060
650-879-0480
www.harleyfarms.com

HOURS: 11–5, daily

Tours each weekend

DESCRIPTION: This is a great escape to the country, and it's not far from San Francisco or the Pacific Coast. It's a charming farmstead operation, and not only can you taste the cheese, buy bath products made with their milk, and visit with the goats, but they also have a beautiful garden where you can see the flowers

that make Harley's cheeses so distinctive. Also, local chefs sometimes host dinners here.

LOLETA CHEESE COMPANY

252 Loleta Drive
Loleta, CA 95551
707-733-5470
www.loletacheese.com

HOURS: 9–5, daily

DESCRIPTION: Not only can you see the cheese being made through viewing windows, but there's a great little shop and a gorgeous garden where you can sip a drink, munch some cheese, or just plain relax. Owner Bob Laffranchi also has plans to build a deli/café into the store sometime in the near future.

MARIN FRENCH CHEESE CO.

7500 Red Hill Road
Petaluma CA, 94952
800-292-6001
www.marinfrenchcheese.com

HOURS: 4:30 AM–5 PM, daily

DESCRIPTION: You might see bicyclists picnicking on the grounds here. Not only is there a great little store, but it's in a beautiful location, right in the midst of some rolling hills and not far from vineyards. The store sells more than just cheese, and viewing windows let you peek in on the cheesemakers hard at work. Group tours can also be arranged.

RINCONADA DAIRY AND BED AND BREAKFAST

4680 West Pozo Road
Santa Margarita, CA 93453
805-438-5667
www.rinconadadairy.com

HOURS: By reservation

DESCRIPTION: This is truly an artisan farmstead operation on a beautiful ranch. But what makes this special isn't only the cheese that Christine Maguire crafts by hand from her herds of sheep and goats: You can spend the night here, too. This two-room bed and breakfast offers the perfect country getaway. Gardens, tastefully decorated rooms, and gourmet breakfasts await.

SPRING HILL JERSEY CHEESE CO./ PETALUMA CREAMERY

FARM: 4235 Spring Hill Road
CREAMERY: 621 Western Avenue
Petaluma CA 94952
707-762-3446
www.springhillcheese.com

HOURS: 10–5, daily

DESCRIPTION: The Petaluma Creamery store is a charming little store with an ice cream and coffee bar. It's a great place to buy cheese, get a quick nibble, or pick up some gifts to bring home. The farm itself opens its doors wide every October for its Peter Pumpkin festival— you can dig for potatoes, pick your pumpkins, milk cows, and enjoy ice cream right there on the farm.

VELLA CHEESE COMPANY

315 Second Street East
Sonoma, CA. 95476
800-848-0505
www.vellacheese.com

HOURS: 9:30–6, Monday through Saturday

DESCRIPTION: Just off the square in downtown Sonoma, this landmark was originally a brewery. It's a gorgeous old building, and it serves up some of the best cheese in the state.

WINCHESTER CHEESE COMPANY

32605 Holland Road
Winchester, CA 92596
951-926-4239
www.winchestercheese.com

HOURS: 9–5, Monday through Friday; 10–4, Saturday through Sunday

DESCRIPTION: The only creamery that is housed in a series of trailers that actually have current license plates is worth a visit. Besides its amazing Gouda, the store itself is charming and offers more than just cheese.

CALL-AHEAD VISITS OR SPECIAL EVENTS

BY APPOINTMENT

ACHADINHA CHEESE COMPANY

750 Chileno Valley Road
Petaluma, CA 94952
707-763-1025
www.achadinha.com

DESCRIPTION: Donna and Jim Pacheco have plans to open a creamery and visitor's center on their farm in 2009, but call ahead to see if construction is complete. Donna is also frequently involved with local food events, so call to find out where she might be.

DÉLICE DE LA VALLÉE/ THE EPICUREAN CONNECTION

P.O. Box 1916
Sonoma, CA 95476
707-935-7960
sheana@vom.com
www.sheanadavis.com

DESCRIPTION: Chef, cheesemaker, and culinary educator Sheana Davis does much more than make cheese. She also often teaches, hosts events, and caters. Call to find out what she's got on her calendar.

SHARON BICE

Redwood Hill's head cheesemaker, Erika Scharfen, shows off some of her gorgeous wheels.

MID-COAST CHEESE COMPANY (FRANKLIN'S TELEME)

P.O. Box 2456
Los Banos, CA 93635
209-826-6259
www.franklinscheese.com

DESCRIPTION: While Franklin Peluso can't open the doors of his creamery to the public, he's often right out there, at grocery stores, culinary events, and other occasions, offering tastes of his great cheese. Check his Web site or call to find out where he's going to be next.

POINT REYES FARMSTEAD CHEESE

14700 Highway 1
Point Reyes Station, CA 94956
4145-663-8880
www.pointreyescheese.com

DESCRIPTION: The new creamery will have an education center, and classes will be some of the many events hosted at the farmstead creamery. Since the Giacomini family also loves to cook—and they've even published a cookbook with recipes for their addictive blue cheese—they also will likely be hosting some culinary events, too. And since they are located almost right next to Tomales Bay, there's a great ocean breeze that comes by the farm.

REDWOOD HILL FARM
AND CREAMERY

2064 Highway 116 North, Building 1, Suite 130
Sebastopol, CA 95472
707-823-8250
www.redwoodhill.com

DESCRIPTION: Every year this creamery hosts farm days, and people are invited to come not only to the creamery, but also to the farm to visit with the goats. Check the Web site for this fabulous annual event.

SOLEDAD GOATS

6501 Backus Road
Mojave, CA 93501
661-824-4514

DESCRIPTION: Carol and Julian Pierce welcome visitors to meet their goats, but you must call ahead—they're a small operation, and they're often at farmers' markets throughout the week so you don't want to stop by when they're not there.

Soledad also sells soap made with the milk of their goats.

CHAPTER 13

Where to Stay, Where to Eat, and What to See

WHILE VISITING

California isn't a small state, by any means, and the cheesemakers aren't located in any one region of California. That's one reason it's such a great state for cheese, but this same diversity of *terroir* means that you can't visit all of your favorite cheesemakers in just one weekend or even a week.

You will need to drive a car to visit cheesemakers, and if you are coming from another region of the country or even the same state, you'll probably need to fly in. San Francisco, Los Angeles, and Eureka are all jumping off points (Eureka for Loleta). The appendix on day trips suggests some groupings of cheesemakers.

But while you're out visiting cheesemakers, you might want to take in the sights, spend an overnight or two in a cozy or hip hotel, and definitely enjoy some of the fine, fine California cuisine and great wines. This chapter will offer some suggestions of places to stay, eat, and visit.

EUREKA / HUMBOLDT COUNTY

Though there's only one cheesemaker open (just about every day of the year) to visitors here, it's worth a special trip, not just because Loleta Cheese is wonderful, but because this is the only place in the world like it. Thousands of thousand- and hundred-year-old giant redwoods beckon. There are also charming towns, the Pacific Coast, and even some wineries in the area. Worth a visit is downtown Ferndale with its Victorian buildings, shops, and galleries (it was featured in the Jim Carrey movie *The Majestic*). Not to mention some amazing cuisine and some of the greenest pastures you'll ever see, along with happy cows, goats, and sheep munching on said pastures. They also have an annual Bigfoot festival. For more information, do check out http://redwoods.info.

CARTER HOUSE INNS

301 L Street
Eureka, CA 95501
800-404-1390
www.carterhouse.com

COST: $195 and up

CREDIT CARDS: MC, V, D, AE

DESCRIPTION: Innkeepers Mark and Christi Carter know how to treat a guest. The AAA Four Diamond rated Carter House Inns and Restaurant 301, which features four Victorian inns practically adjacent to Humboldt Bay, is plush, welcoming, and one of the nicest places to stay, with fireplaces, whirlpool tubs, and private decks, among other stunning amenities. From

Carter House Inns are an absolutely charming place to vacation.

the wine welcome and appetizers in the evening to a gourmet three-course breakfast in the morning, no detail goes unnoticed. The restaurant features an extensive cheese and wine list, and because Mark is not only an innkeeper but a Napa Valley vintner, it also boasts some of his amazing wines. Pets are also welcome.

LEFT: *Carter House Inns boast a private garden where visitors can relax.* RIGHT: *Some suites feature a full kitchen.*

While in Napa, it's also recommended that you stop and visit Mark's Carter Cellars, www.cartercellars.com.

THE VICTORIAN INN

400 Ocean Avenue
Ferndale, CA
707-786-4949
www.A-Victorian-Inn.com

COST: $105 and up

CREDIT CARDS: MC, V, D, AE

DESCRIPTION: Charming and cozy, The Victorian Inn is a wonderful place to stay if you also plan on visiting the equally charming town of Ferndale. Restored to its historical detail by owners Lowell Daniels and Jenny Oaks, this is a place to step back into yesteryear, while maintaining all of the luxe amenities one would expect in the 21st Century; some rooms boast a whirlpool. Lowell and Jenny welcome guests with a Humboldt County wine and cheese tasting, and breakfasts are sumptuous. Curley Tait is the inn's signature restaurant, and it's one of the best places to eat in the county.

SAMOA COOKHOUSE

Across the Samoa Bridge
Off Cookhouse Road
Samoa, California 95564
707-442-1659
www.samoacookhouse.net

COST: Inexpensive

DESCRIPTION: There aren't too many lumberjack jobs left in the West, but you can still eat like one. This is the oldest logging camp cookhouse in the West, dating back 115 years, and it's a step back into history They serve breakfast, lunch, and dinner, family style every day of the year, and the food—all made from scratch, including salad dressings and bread—is absolutely fantastic.

RESTAURANT 301
301 L Street
Eureka, CA 95501
800-404-1390

COST: Expensive

DESCRIPTION: Elegant, gourmet, and delicious, this is one of the finest restaurants in northern California. Plus one of the best wine lists around.

HUMBOLDT REDWOODS STATE PARK
P.O. Box 100
Weott, CA 95571
707-946-2409
www.humboldtredwood.org

DESCRIPTION: The 32-mile long Avenue of the Giants parallels Highway 101, and there are several on-ramps throughout the drive. The park itself covers more than 52,000 acres, 17,000 of which are some of the oldest growth coastal redwoods in the world. "These are our cathedrals," says Loleta Cheese's Bob Laffranchi, and he's absolutely right. They're one of those things you definitely need to see at least once in your life. Plus, if you've ever watched *Return of the Jedi*, this is where the Ewoks lived.

The redwoods are even taller up close.

SAN FRANCISCO

UNION SQUARE HOTEL
114 Powell Street
San Francisco, CA 94102
414-397-3000
www.hotelunionsquare.com

COST: $149 and up

CREDIT CARDS: MC, V, D, AE

DESCRIPTION: One of the Personality Hotels in San Francisco, this boutique hotel was constructed back in 1913, and it was a favorite place of *Maltese Falcon* writer Dashiell Hammett. Just last year it underwent a stunning renovation, and it's a visually stimulating blend of classic San Francisco and modern design. Sleek furnishings, 600-thread-count linens, and more await.

HALF MOON BAY INN
401 Main Street
Half Moon Bay, CA 94019
650-726-1177
www.halfmoonbayinn.com

COST: $120 and up

CREDIT CARDS: MC, V, D, AE

DESCRIPTION: This darling inn boasts 600-thread-count linens, quiet rooms, and suites, some with whirlpool baths. Built on what was once a blacksmith shop, the inn has a historic feel to it, but it's definitely modern in its décor and amenities; its bath products, for example, are made by a local bath store in town. Dogs are welcome.

CETRELLA
845 Main Street
Half Moon Bay, CA 94019
650-726-4090

COST: Expensive

DESCRIPTION: Locally grown ingredients are served up with a Mediterranean flair. The wood oven-roasted salmon and the roasted rack of lamb are to-die-for delicious, and their baked focaccia, made with Bellwether Farms Crescenza is something you'll dream of for days after consuming it. Extensive wine and cheese list to boot.

Cetrella is as charming as its food is delicious.

A fireplace welcomes guests on chilly nights at Cetrella.

SONOMA COUNTY

The second-largest wine region in the country is also close to many of California's artisan cheesemakers. It's a gorgeous place to visit if you like to eat and drink, and there are tons of things to see and do. For more information, you can contact the Russian River Wine Road, 800-723-6336, www.wineroad.com.

HOPE-MERRILL HOUSE

P.O. Box 42
Geyserville, CA 95441
800.825.4233
http://hope-inns.com

COST: $149 and up

CREDIT CARDS: MC, V, D, AE

DESCRIPTION: Two darling Victorian inns, plus an in-ground pool, are a welcoming retreat. Not only do they boast tastefully appointed rooms, but they also host an annual winemaking event: two weekends a year in which guests come to harvest and process the grapes, and then return to mix and bottle the wine. Gourmet breakfasts also await. Children are welcome, too.

FOUNTAINGROVE INN

101 Fountaingrove Parkway
Santa Rosa, CA 95403
800-222-6101
www.fountaingroveinn.com

COST: $188 and up

CREDIT CARDS: MC, V, D, AE

DESCRIPTION: This AAA Four Diamond rated hotel has a conference center, pool, restaurant, and workout room, not to mention plush, comfortable rooms. The contemporary hotel features complimentary bottled water, cookies and coffee in the afternoon, and continental breakfast, too.

HONOR MANSION

14891 Grove Street
Healdsburg, CA 95448
707-433-4277
www.honormansion.com

COST: $190 and up

CREDIT CARDS: MC, V, D, AE

DESCRIPTION: Walking grounds, bocce courts, a

swimming pool, and private, enclosed porches with Jacuzzis await at this AAA Four Diamond inn. Full, gourmet breakfasts and gourmet wine and appetizers in the evenings also make this a worthwhile stay for foodies.

MADRONA MANOR
1001 Westside Road
Healdsburg, CA 95448
800-258-4003
www.madronamanor.com

COST: Expensive

DESCRIPTION: The food here is simply stunning, and each course can be appropriately paired with a local wine to match. Chef Jesse Mallgren and his able staff create seasonal menus that are quite memorable. Anything on the menu is good, but do order the tableside ice cream for dessert—it's the only ice cream dish in which your waiter will make the ice cream right in front of you, and it's not only worth it for the theatrical aspect, it's so, so good. Besides the restaurant, you can also stay here at the inn, too.

There are a ton of wineries to visit in Sonoma County. Here are four of my favorites:

COPAIN WINERY
www.copainwines.com

KENDALL JACKSON WINE CENTER GARDENS
www.kj.com/home.asp

PARADISE RIDGE WINERY
www.paradiseridgewinery.com

SEGHESIO FAMILY VINEYARDS
(for tasting, bocce, and oven-baked pizza)
www.seghesio.com

To better enjoy the wine or cheese, I suggest taking a hot air balloon or a bike ride. Both get you up close and personal with the vineyards and the pastures, but from two different vantage points:

UP & AWAY HOT AIR BALLOON
800-711-2998
www.up-away.com

DESCRIPTION: Outside of having to get up before the crack of dawn, this is one of those experiences of a lifetime, and it's so peaceful and gorgeous riding in a balloon, seeing the pastures, vineyards, and beautiful countryside. Afterward, you're rewarded with an outdoor champagne brunch.

WINE COUNTRY BIKES

61 Front Street
Healdsburg CA 95448
707-473-0610
http://winecountrybikes.com

DESCRIPTION: You can rent bikes for a couple hours, a day, or longer, and the able staff will help you set up a bike and a route that you're comfortable with.

NAPA COUNTY

LA RESIDENCE

4066 Howard Lane
Napa, CA 94558
800-253-9203
www.laresidence.com

COST: $199 and up

CREDIT CARDS: MC, V, D, AE

DESCRIPTION: Four secluded buildings are tucked away in the heart of wine country. Furnished with antiques, plush linens, flat screen televisions, and more, this is an amazing place to stay. Also, a heated outdoor pool and hot tub to relax in, wine and appetizer receptions in the evening, plus gourmet three-course breakfasts in the morning.

LOS ANGELES

VENICE BEACH ECO COTTAGES

447 Grand Boulevard
Venice, CA 90291
866-802-3110
www.venicebeachecocottages.com

COST: $215/night, 2-night minimum

CREDIT CARDS: MC, V, D, AE

DESCRIPTION: Three solar-powered cottages offer green yet deluxe accommodations in the heart of Venice, just blocks from the beach. Cynthia Foster and Karel Samsom took these cottages, which were ready to be demolished, and they completely remodeled them using only sustainable materials and resources. Each one is quaint yet modern, and their interior design is just stunning. Dogs welcome.

The swivel chair in this cottage is made from a recycled bird cage.

LEFT AND RIGHT: *La Residence is a quiet, comfortable retreat.*

PRIMITIVO WINE BAR

1025 Abbot Kinney Boulevard
Venice, CA 90291
310-396-5353

COST: Mid-priced

DESCRIPTION: This funky bistro serves up amazing tapas and entrees, along with, of course, a killer wine list. It's just a few blocks from the eco cottages, and it is warm, relaxing, and fun. The bacon-wrapped fig appetizer is to die for.

APPENDIXES

DAY TRIPS FOR VISITING CHEESEMAKERS

*I*f you are planning to visit California's cheesemakers and dairy artisans, you probably should plan on spending anywhere from one to three hours per cheesemaker, and ideally, you can probably only visit three to four in a day, max. And, yes, you likely will be doing a lot of driving if you plan to visit the cheesemakers in California who accept visitors!

If you are using San Francisco as a base, you can drive down to Harley Farms for a day trip, perhaps spending the night or afternoon in charming Half Moon Bay, nearby. If you're in San Francisco on a Saturday, head down to the Ferry Plaza Building for a fantastic farmers' market, and there you can meet a plethora of cheese and dairy masters including St. Benoît's and Andante. You can also drive up to Sonoma County for a day, and I also recommend using Sonoma County as a jumping-off point to visit several cheesemakers. While you're there, do check out the wineries, too.

Sonoma and Marin counties are adjacent, and they are home to a large selection of artisan cheese-makers. In Marin, you could visit Cowgirl Creamery and Marin County French; if Point Reyes is hosting an event, you could also fit them in.

In Sonoma, check out Vella and Springhill Jersey together; also, if Achadinha is open, you could also fit

CYPRESS GROVE CHÈVE

The milk for Cypress Grove's cheese comes from local family farms.

them in, as well as Redwood Hill, if they are hosting their farm days when you are in town. Though Pug's Leap doesn't accept visitors, you can find them every Saturday morning at the Healdsburg Farmer's Market, and that is worth a visit in itself (Springhill Jersey also is at that same market). And see if Sheana Davis is conducting any events while you're in Sonoma, too.

If you are using Los Angeles as a jumping off point, you can check out Soledad or Winchester, but not both in the same day. You can also drive from Los Angeles to visit Rinconada, but as it is a four-hour drive, you will definitely want to spend the night at Rinconada.

The Healdsburg Farmers' Market is a delight for the senses.

Fagundes, Bravo, and Fiscalini are all sort of between San Francisco and Los Angeles so you can take your pick as to which city you'd prefer as a jumping-off point. But they're not exactly close together so you'd have to drive a ways if you tried to include all three in a single day.

Loleta is a trip all by itself to far northern California, but it's a trip everyone should make at least once in their lives, to see the redwoods. Also, sometimes Cypress Grove and Humboldt Creamery do host events or attend cheese-related events in the county, but those are rather rare.

SHOPPING FOR CALIFORNIA CHEESE AND DAIRY PRODUCTS

**THE CHEESE STORE
OF BEVERLY HILLS**
419 N. Beverly Drive
Beverly Hills, CA 90210
310-278-2855
www.cheesestorebh.com

THE CHEESE SHOP
423 Center Street
Healdsburg, CA 95448
707-433-4998
www.doraliceimports.com

CHEESETIQUE ARTISAN CHEESE SHOP
2403 Mount Vernon Avenue
Alexandria, VA 22301
703-706-5300
www.cheesetique.com

HALF MOON BAY WINE & CHEESE
Half Moon Bay, CA
604 Main Street
650-726-1520
www.hmbwineandcheese.com

JIMTOWN STORE
6706 State Highway 128
Healdsburg, CA 95448
707-433-1212
www.jimtown.com

LARRY'S MARKET
8737 N. Deerwood Drive
Brown Deer, WI 53209
414-355-9650
www.larrysmarket.com

MARION STREET CHEESE MARKET
101 N. Marion Street
Oak Park, IL 60301
708-848-2088
www.marionstreetcheesemarket.com

MURRAY'S CHEESE
254 Bleecker Street
New York, NY 10014
212-243-3289
www.murrayscheese.com

PASTORAL ARTISAN CHEESE STORE
2945 N. Broadway Street
Chicago, IL 60657
773-472-4781
www.pastoralartisan.com

PETALUMA MARKET
210 Western Avenue
Petaluma, CA 94952
707-762-8452
www.petalumamarket.com

PREMIER CHEESE MARKET
5013 France Avenue S.
Minneapolis, MN 55410
612-436-5590
www.premiercheesemarket.com

ZINGERMAN'S
2501 Jackson Avenue
Ann Arbor, MI 48103
888-636-8162
www.zingermans.com

RESOURCES FOR BUDDING CHEESEMAKERS

AMERICAN CHEESE SOCIETY
304 W. Liberty Street, Suite 201
Louisville, KY 40202
502-583-3783
www.cheesesociety.org

**BUTTER COMMUNICATIONS/
LYNNE DEVEREUX**
925-872-6691
www.buttercommunications.com

CALIFORNIA ARTISAN CHEESE GUILD
P.O. Box 184
Guerneville, CA 95446
info@cacheeseguild.org
www.cacheeseguild.org

CALIFORNIA MILK ADVISORY BOARD
400 Oyster Point Boulevard, Suite 211
South San Francisco, CA 94090
650-871-6455
www.realcaliforniamilk.com

**THE CHEESE IMPRESARIO/
BARRIE LYNN**
barrielynn@thecheeseimpresario.com
www.thecheeseimpresario.com

CHEESE SCHOOL OF SAN FRANCISCO
2155 Powell Street
San Francisco, CA 94133
415-346-7530
www.cheeseschoolsf.com

**NEW ENGLAND CHEESE MAKING
SUPPLY**
P.O. Box 85
Ashfield, MA 01330
413-628-3808
www.cheesemaking.com

**SHEANA DAVIS, EPICUREAN
CONNECTION**
P.O. Box 1916
Sonoma, CA 95476
707-935-7960
www.sheanadavis.com

CALIFORNIA
WINE AND CHEESE PAIRINGS

heese and wine go together like peanut butter and jelly, Bert and Ernie, Lennon and McCartney, Laverne and Shirley . . . you get the picture. And why wouldn't they? As cheese is oft considered "the wine of food," they naturally go together. But wine isn't the only beverage that one can enjoy with cheese, and some say that beer goes even better with cheese. You can even pair cheese with tea, coffee, and spirits, too. In the last several years that I have been investigating the mystical pairings conundrum, I've learned that there's much debate on the topic, and for every pairing "rule" you can come up with, there's always an exception.

That said, there still are some good basics to know if you plan on setting up a wine and cheese tasting or a cheese and beverage tasting, and in any pairing, you're trying to balance the flavors of the beverage with the flavors of the cheese. "Cheese will affect wine more than wine will affect cheese," says Lynne Devereux, president of the California Artisan Cheese Guild.

Wine has about 700 or so chemical compounds that affect taste, while cheese has about 200 or so compounds that affect taste, and in pairings, you're trying to get these tastes to match up. One good rule to follow when you're just starting is to choose a wine with low tannins. Tannins are the chemical compounds (phenols) that cause your mouth to pucker when you sip a wine, and they're found in the skins, seeds, and stems of grapes, which means they are only found in red wines. "They cause that fuzzy feeling in your mouth after drinking a cup of tea," explains Gretchen Roberts, noted wine writer. Tannins also help preserve wines, and as wines age, they add to their complexity of flavors. They also have an effect on proteins when you eat them, and cheeses, as you may know, are a good source of protein. "Tannins and milk don't go well together," Gretchen says.

What I've found is that heavily tannic wines like Bordeaux or cabernet sauvignon tend not to mesh as well with cheeses. It's also for this reason that heavily oaked chardonnays tend to clash more with cheeses. "Oak has a bitterness to it," Lynne says.

That's why, whereas many magazines might publish photos of red wine with cheese because the redness pops in the picture, they might not be the best choice for pairing with cheese. "The reason I think people tend to think of red wine with cheese is that cheese is a dessert course, and in Europe, you start with a light wine at the beginning of a meal, and you progress to heavier wines," Gretchen says. "The custom is that you're on red wine with the meal, and then you finish that off with a cheese course, but it really is okay to switch back to a white after dinner if you're doing a cheese course."

If you do prefer red wines to white wines, go for the food-friendly pinot noirs or Beaujolais. "You want wines that are fruit forward with a nice balance," Lynne says. They're lighter, less tannic, and more likely not to clash. Dry rosés also tend to fall into the more food-friendly category, too (and, as a note, white zinfandel is not a rosé, and to many oenophiles, it's not even considered a wine). That's important if you're tasting a wide range of cheeses. Heavier red wines, however, do go with stronger, more aged cheeses. An aged Gouda or really, really rich Camembert will more likely stand up to a stronger wine.

White wines, as a general rule, as they are lighter and often fruitier, pair up more immediately with a wider array of cheeses than red wines. White wines have more acidity than red wines, and the acidity can lift the cheese and cleanse the palate. Rieslings tend to be my go-to wine if I'm not sure what cheeses I'm having. They tend to mesh beautifully with an array of cheeses, and the cheeses tend to tone down their sweetness, and as someone who prefers drier wines, that is a good thing. "Rieslings are so versatile because they're slightly sweet, acidic, fragrant, and floral, and if you don't know what kind of cheese you're having, there will be some quality in the Riesling that will complement it," Gretchen says.

Another type of wine that goes with almost any kind of cheese is sparkling wine or champagne. They're just heavenly with bloomy rind cheeses like Brie, and their effervescence lifts and cleanses the palate.

Also, sweet wines tend to go amazingly well with many cheeses. Gewürztraminers, muscats, and ports tend to go well with salty, strong cheeses. In fact, they traditionally have been paired up with blue cheeses for centuries. The saltiness of the blues contrast beautifully with the sweetness of the wines. This illustrates another rule of pairings—contrasting flavors sometimes harmonize. One interesting way to serve up this specific pairing is to put dabs of blue cheese in individual Asian soup spoons, pour a bit of wine over the cheese, and enjoy.

Another important aspect when pairing wines with cheese is to consider the condiments you plan on serving with them. "Condiments act as a bridge between the wine and the cheese," says Barrie Lynn, consultant and president of The Cheese Impresario in Los Angeles. Honeys, jams, olive oils, and even cracked pepper can be added to the cheese.

The sweetness of honeys, jams, preserves, and chutneys can bridge the fruitiness of the wine with the cheese. Cracked pepper, Barrie says, is especially helpful when trying to pair cheeses with red wines because the pepper will pick up the, well, peppery notes, of the wine and make the wine and cheese meld more harmoniously. Although it was a bit unusual the first time I cracked pepper onto my cheese before sipping my red wine, I noticed that it made a big difference, and the wine did match up with the cheese so much better. I was really amazed, and if you prefer red wines, then this is one tip you'll want to hang onto.

Another interesting condiment, which Lynne suggests, is to soak golden raisins in olorosa sherry, and then spoon the mixture over an aged cheese like Winchester's super aged Gouda. The sweetness of the California raisins and the sherry cut through the strength of the cheese.

Another way to approach cheeses is to go the traditional route. In Europe, many times, whatever cheese was crafted in a region naturally goes with whatever wines are cultivated in that area. For example, many of the famed French goat's milk cheeses in the Loire Valley tend to pair up very well with the Vouvrays and Sancerres that the Loire is known for. Chianti also tends to go very well with fresh mozzarella, and big Tuscan red wines often go beautifully with aged pecorinos.

You can almost do the same thing with California wines and California cheeses. But just as cheese types aren't restricted by geography in the United States, neither are wine types. In just the Sonoma Valley, you can find amazing zinfandels, pinot noirs, sauvignon blancs, cabernet sauvignons, chardonnays, and more. You can also find triple crèmes, fresh chèvres, Bries, Dry Jacks, and more. So the diversity of the wines and cheeses produced within California's distinct *terroirs* doesn't mean that they will immediately pair up.

Beer also goes quite well with cheese, and there was even a seminar at the last American Cheese Society conference entitled "Beer and Wine Smackdown." At that seminar the audience was evenly divided, and the final verdict, it seems, was that the beer lovers preferred beer with cheese and the wine lovers preferred wine with cheese. Overall, one versatile beer for cheese is hefeweizen. Hard ciders also work very well with many cheeses. Hoppy beers go well with blue cheeses while pale ales tend to cut through the richness of really aged cheeses.

Here are a few suggested cheese and wine or beer pairings:

DRY JACK—pinot noir, Belgian-style ale
BRIES—champagne, kir royale, apple or pear hard cider
MEDIUM OR MILD GOUDAS—buttery chardonnays, nut brown ales, or creamy stouts
MONTEREY JACK—Rieslings, gruner veltliners, nut brown ales
CHEDDARS—Ruby ports, bold rich stouts
CHÈVRES—sauvignon blanc, Sancerre, mild pilsners
BLUE—Port, zinfandel, a porter ale, or lambic (fruity) beer

If you're interested in more specific pairings, do visit the Web sites of the cheesemakers you enjoy, as some of them, like Cypress Grove, have suggested pairings. Also, here are four Web sites for pairing suggestions: Everyday Wine, www.everydaywine.net; Gourmet Sleuth, www.gourmetsleuth.com/cpairing.htm; Nat Decants, www.nataliemaclean.com; and Lucy Saunders, www.beercook.com.

Keep in mind that different vintages or brews of wine or beer can taste very differently, especially from year to year, and the main thing when pairing is to drink and eat what you like. Ultimately, it is your taste buds that matter, so first and foremost, go with what you enjoy.

CHEESE FLIGHTS
AND TASTING PLATES

Tasting the cheese you've been reading about is the best part, and there are so many wonderful California cheeses to enjoy. When I set up a flight or tasting plate of cheeses for friends or family members, there are two basic techniques I employ: horizontal and vertical tastings.

A horizontal tasting is the more traditional sort of cheese tasting. It's basically a variety of cheeses of different tastes, textures, and types. A typical horizontal tasting will include a variety of cheesemakers, milks, and colors. Usually I will select between three and eight different cheeses, and I serve them mild to strong, with blue always served last. Most experts don't recommend more than four to six, but if you are serving small portions, I've enjoyed as many as a dozen, for example, at the Carter House Inns in Eureka.

One example of a California horizontal tasting is: Soledad lemon and lavender chèvre, Délice de la Vallée, Marin French Gold Brie, Winchester medium Gouda, Three Sisters Serena, Fiscalini's bandaged cheddar, and Point Reyes Blue.

A vertical tasting, however, is when you take a single cheese and either serve a variety of the same cheese made by different cheesemakers, or the same type but of different ages made by the same cheesemaker. For example, set up a California chèvre tasting—include fresh chèvres made by Laura Chenel, Redwood Hill, Cypress Grove, and Soledad. Or include a variety of goat's milk cheeses, from fresh chèvres to Pug's Leap's bloomy rinds to Rinconada's Pozo Tomme and Cypress Grove's Humboldt Fog. Or, set up a Monterey Jack tasting, with jacks from Vella, Fagundes, and Springhill Jersey.

You can also set up a tasting of the same cheese, but at different ages. It would be really fun to do this with all of the Goudas that Winchester makes.

Just as there are two basic ways to set up a tasting, there are two basic ways to serve tastings. The first, and probably easiest way, is to arrange the tasting on one or two platters, and have your guests serve themselves. The second is to serve small portions of each cheese on plates for all of your guests. A good rule of thumb is to serve about 2 to 4 ounces of cheese per guest, and buy the cheese the day of or the day before you are planning to serve it.

Let the cheese warm up to room temperature before you serve it, and when you plate the cheese, always keep the washed rinds and blues either on a separate plate or distinctly sep-

arated on the plates from the other cheeses. Also, if you are putting out a single platter of cheese, make sure you have an individual knife for each cheese.

Be sure to serve the cheese with crusty baguettes and crackers, along with some dried or fresh fruits and nuts. In general, plain and unflavored breads work best, but fruit and nut breads also complement cheese. Fresh berries, dried cranberries, cherries and apricots, fresh or dried figs, and sliced apples work well, as do almonds, hazelnuts, walnuts, and pecans,

California makes a variety of delicious dairy products.

173

spiced or just lightly toasted. Olives also go well with cheeses. For California-only tastings, I especially love using California produce like strawberries, kiwis, and olives.

Jams, marmalades, and honey can also be drizzled over the cheese or placed out for your guests to dab on their cheeses. Port wine and balsamic vinegar can be good, too, and port is especially good for blue cheeses.

When I am setting up a cheese plate for a party, I usually like to go to one of my favorite local stores and taste the cheese before I purchase it. A good cheese merchant or maitre *fromager* at a quality restaurant can introduce you to new finds or help you discover new ways of pairing old favorites. If you have a good cheese store in your area that sells California cheeses, get to know the staff there. If California cheeses or the specific California cheeses you're craving aren't sold within your area, most cheesemakers either sell them direct on the Internet or over the phone, and there are some great stores that will also ship them to you.

It is best to eat your good cheeses within the week that you purchase them. Store them in your vegetable drawer (free of vegetables, of course), and if you need to wrap them up again after eating, use clean (not used) plastic, foil, or wax paper, or store them in a nice plastic or glass container.

I've also seen it suggested that you rub (except for blue cheeses) the cheeses with extra virgin olive oil before you wrap them up to better preserve them, but I haven't personally tried that (cheese generally does not last long in my house). Many experts say wax paper works best, but the main rule is to not overbuy and then have the cheese go bad in your refrigerator. Also, never store washed rinds or blues in the same container. And if you have a bunch of different cheeses left over, try making homemade cheese spread (there's a recipe for that in the recipe section.)

RECIPES FOR CALIFORNIA CHEESE

FROMAGE FORT OR HOMEMADE CHEESE SPREAD
(WHAT TO DO WITH LEFTOVER CHEESE)

⅓ to ½ pound leftover cheese
2 sticks of unsalted butter, softened
½ cup white wine
2–3 big cloves of garlic
salt, white pepper to taste

Place all ingredients in a food processor except salt and pepper. Chop until finely mixed. If it is not creamy enough, add a drizzle more of wine or a little more butter. Then add seasonings; be careful about adding salt since cheese has a lot of salt in it. *Makes about 2 cups cheese spread.*

TAMARA'S BRIE

Triangle of Brie, usually a double or triple crème Brie
¾ cup shelled, unsalted, roasted pistachios
1 cup fresh raspberries

Preheat oven to 400 degrees F. Put Brie in a nonstick baking pan or dish. Pour pistachios over Brie, letting them stick to the sides of the cheese. Bake for about 10 to 12 minutes. When it starts melting and getting a little bit oozy, pour the raspberries on top, and bake for an additional 2 to 3 minutes. Serve with slices of crusty bread. *Makes 4 to 6 appetizer servings.*

GRILLED FIG SALAD
POINT REYES BLUE

SALAD

½ cup pancetta

12 fresh figs, halved

    10 to 12 cups loosely packed mixed greens

1 cup chopped, toasted walnuts

1 cup Point Reyes Blue cheese crumbles

PORT VINAIGRETTE

3 dried figs

1 cup ruby port

¼ cup red wine vinegar

2 tsp minced shallots

⅔ cup extra virgin olive oil

    salt and pepper to taste

TO PREPARE THE SALAD: Sauté pancetta in a small skillet over medium-high heat until crisp. Drain but reserve drippings. Set aside. Brush figs with reserved pancetta drippings and grill figs for about 1 minute on each side. (May broil if desired.) In a large bowl, toss the greens, walnuts, cheese, and reserved pancetta with port vinaigrette. Place salad mixture on plates and surround with figs.

TO PREPARE THE VINAIGRETTE: Combine figs and port in small saucepan. Simmer until port reduces to ½ cup. In a blender or processor, purée fig and port mixture with vinegar. Stir in shallots and slowly whisk in oil until emulsified. Season with salt and pepper to taste.

ASPARAGUS SOUP WITH POINT REYES BLUE
POINT REYES BLUE

½ cup butter
1 large onion, sliced
1 large leek, thinly sliced
½ pound potatoes, cubed
6 cups low-salt chicken broth
1½ lbs chopped asparagus, woody ends removed
salt, pepper to taste
⅔ cup Point Reyes Original Blue crumbles

Melt butter in large saucepan over medium heat. Add onion and cook 1 to 2 minutes. Add leek, potato cubes, and broth. Bring to a boil, then reduce to simmer until potatoes are tender. Add asparagus. Simmer until asparagus is just tender, about 4 to 5 minutes. Remove from heat; in food processor or blender, purée soup until it is smooth. Return to saucepan over low heat, season to taste. To serve, pour in bowls and top with blue cheese crumbles. *Makes 4 servings.*

POLENTA WITH THREE SISTERS SERENA
THREE SISTERS

7 cups water
1 Tbsp salt
2 cups polenta
1 oz unsalted butter
¼ cup Swiss cheese, grated
¼ cup Serena, grated
½ tsp jalapeño purée
¼ cup fresh basil or chives, chopped

Bring the water to a boil in a big pot. Add salt, then stir in polenta in a steady stream, stirring constantly. After all polenta is absorbed, stir until polenta pulls away from the sides of the pan. Add butter, cheeses, and jalapeño purée. Stir in basil or chives just before serving. *Makes about 8 servings.*

WOOD-OVEN-BAKED FOCACCIA

EXECUTIVE CHEF GREGORY HUTCHINSON, CETRELLA RESTAURANT, HALF MOON BAY

8 ounces pizza dough, divided into two portions
1–2 Tbsp extra virgin olive oil
3 ounces Crescenza cheese
truffle oil

Preheat oven to 450 degrees. With a rolling pin, roll out each of the dough balls until they are very thin, about ¼ of an inch thick or less. Brush olive oil on the bottom of one dough flat, the side that you would lay on the baking sheet or pizza stone. Spread cheese on one dough flat, leaving about ¼-inch edge all around that is free of cheese. Add the other piece of flattened dough on top. Tap the edges and press in with your fingers to make sure the dough is completely sealed all around. Press down gently on the top to push out any air. Bake for 8 minutes on a pizza stone or baking sheet. Drizzle with truffle oil and serve immediately.

GOAT CHEESE AND ROASTED VEGETABLE TERRINE
Executive Chef John Stevenson, The Rose Group properties,
Guastavino's, and 583 Park Avenue, New York City

- 1 cup heavy cream
- 3 Tbsp gelatin
- 1 lb fresh goat cheese (thick and creamy)
- 1 bunch or 2 to 3 tablespoons fresh chopped chervil
  salt, black pepper, sugar to taste
- 1 lb red peppers
- 10 spears asparagus, jumbo size
- 3 portabella mushrooms, large size
- 1 Tbsp fresh garlic, chopped
- 2 lbs leeks, cleaned

EQUIPMENT:
- 1 piping bag
- 1 ceramic terrine mold, about 1-quart size
- 1 large pot of boiling salted water

TO PREPARE THE GOAT CHEESE: In a double boiler, over medium heat, warm the cream and let the gelatin dissolve into it. Remove from heat and add goat cheese, chopped chervil, and season with salt, black pepper and sugar to taste. Place in piping bag until ready for use.

TO PREPARE THE VEGETABLES: Roast red peppers on an open flame until charred (not burnt) using no oil to prevent flames and unwanted smoke residue. If no flame is available, broil in oven. When cooked, place in container and cover with plastic until cooled. When cooled, remove charred skin and seeds. Cut into quarters and dry on a towel. Trim the bottoms of the asparagus and discard. In boiling salted water, quickly blanch the asparagus and shock in ice water. Dry on towel. Clean the portabella mushrooms by removing the stem and gills from underneath. Coat in olive oil, salt, pepper, and chopped garlic; and roast in oven at 325 degrees F until fully cooked or about 15 minutes. When finished, place on paper towel to absorb excess liquid. Peel apart the leek leaves and rinse with cold water. Quickly blanch in boiling salted water and shock in ice water.

TO ASSEMBLE TERRINE: Take terrine mold and line with dry, blanched leek leaves. Be sure that each leaf is overlapping the next to ensure full enclosure. This is the most important step, and will dictate how well the terrine turns out, for it is the leeks that will keep the shape. Spread an even layer of goat cheese mixture about ½-inch thick. Place, evenly spaced, the asparagus spears and add another layer of cheese evenly. Place a layer of roasted red peppers, then another layer of cheese. Place a layer of roasted portabella mushrooms, then another layer of cheese. Fold the leeks over the top and press firmly and evenly, to ensure that filling creates the exact shape of the mold. Place in refrigerator overnight until set. Remove from terrine mold and cut ¾-inch slices. You should see alternating colors of vegetables and cheese, surrounded by green leeks. *Makes 6 servings. Chef suggests serving with arugula pesto and fried parsnips.*

MAC 'N' CHEESE
EXECUTIVE CHEF RASHON SMITH, LUXE HOTEL RODEO DRIVE, BEVERLY HILLS, CA

- 1½ cups grated Parmesan
- 1½ cups grated white cheddar
- 1½ cups grated Swiss (gruyere)
- ½ cup crumbled blue cheese
- ½ cup crumbled chèvre
- 4 Tbsp unsalted butter
- ¼ cup all-purpose flour
  salt and pepper to taste
- 4½ cups heavy cream
- 1 lb pasta (baby shells or penne)
- 2 cups panko bread crumbs

Reserve 1 cup Parmesan for topping, and mix all cheeses. Cover and chill. Melt 4 tablespoons butter in large saucepan over medium heat. Add flour and stir until mixture turns golden brown, about 4 minutes. Add salt and pepper. Gradually whisk in cream. Simmer until thickened and smooth, stirring often, about 4 minutes. Add cheeses from large bowl. Stir until melted and smooth.

Preheat oven to 375 degrees F. Cook pasta in boiling salted water until tender but firm to bite. Drain. Transfer to large bowl. Pour cheese sauce over; toss. Divide among eight 1¼-cup custard cups. Sprinkle with 1 cup reserved cheese. Place cups on rimmed baking sheet. Sprinkle partially baked, chilled, or just assembled cups with bread crumbs. Bake pasta until beginning to bubble and tops are golden, about 20 minutes. *Makes 8 servings.*

KAREN HURT'S SPICY MEAT LASAGNA

SAUCE

- 1 lb lean ground beef
- ¼ tsp chili powder
- salt, pepper to taste
- 1 Tbsp garlic powder
- 1 white onion, finely chopped
- 2 cloves fresh garlic, chopped
- 3 Tbsp extra virgin olive oil
- 1 can (24 oz) crushed tomatoes with basil
- 1 can (6 oz) tomato paste
- 1 cup red wine
- 3 Tbsp fresh basil, chopped
- 3 Tbsp sugar
- 1 Tbsp dried oregano
- 2 tsp garlic salt
- 1 tsp Italian seasoning
- ½ tsp paprika
- ¼ tsp cayenne pepper

Brown meat with chili powder, salt, pepper, and garlic powder. Drain. Sauté onion and fresh garlic with olive oil over medium-high heat in pot. Add tomatoes, tomato paste, red wine, and all spices. Bring to a simmer and cook for 15 minutes.

CHEESE FILLING

16 oz ricotta
8 oz cottage cheese
2 eggs
2 Tbsp fresh basil, chopped
½ cup shredded Parmesan
½ cup mozzarella, plus 1½ cups mozzarella reserved for topping
1 package lasagna noodles, cooked

Mix ricotta, cottage cheese, and eggs together. Then add in basil, Parmesan, and ½ cup of the mozzarella. Preheat oven to 400 degrees F. In lasagna pan, alternate layers of sauce, noodles, and cheese, and top with remaining 1½ cups mozzarella cheese. Bake for 45 minutes. *Makes 6 to 8 servings.*

BROILED PEACHES OR NECTARINES WITH CRÈME CHANTILLY

½ cup crème fraîche
½ cup heavy cream
1 Tbsp honey or sugar
1 tsp real vanilla extract
2 peaches or nectarines, cut in half
4 Tbsp dark rum
1 tsp cinnamon
vanilla ice cream, optional

In a blender or mixer, whip crème fraîche, heavy cream, honey or sugar, and vanilla until foamy and light. Preheat broiler to high. Put peaches or nectarines in ceramic dish, top with rum and sprinkle with cinnamon. Broil for 6 to 8 minutes or until cooked. Serve with a dollop or two of crème chantilly and a sprinkling of cinnamon. Can also serve with a scoop of vanilla ice cream, too. *Makes 4 servings.*

CRÈME FRAÎCHE SCONES

SADIE KENDALL'S THE CRÈME FRAÎCHE COOKBOOK

- 2 cups cake flour, sifted
- 1 Tbsp sugar
- 2¼ tsp baking powder
- ½ tsp salt
- 1 cup crème fraîche
- sugar for sprinkling

Preheat oven to 450 degrees F. Sift together flour, sugar, baking powder, and salt. Mix crème fraiche into dry ingredients. The mixture should be moist enough that it forms a cohesive dough. If it is too dry, add more crème fraiche, just a little at a time so that it can be more easily handled. Pat dough out onto a pastry board or table that has been lightly floured. Roll or press dough down until it is ¾-inch thick. Cut into desired shapes. Sprinkle with sugar, and bake for 15 to 20 minutes until the scones start to brown. *Makes 10 scones. Serve with Sadie's mascarpone and preserves.*

SADIE'S MASCARPONE

- 1 cup crème fraiche

Line a colander with a clean cloth. Place colander over a bowl. Put crème fraîche into cloth, close cloth, add weight. Let drain for 2 hours at room temperature.

GLOSSARY

ACIDIFICATION: The process in which bacterial cultures affect and change the milk sugar or lactose into lactic acid during cheesemaking. The level of acidity affects the taste of the cheese.

AFFINAGE: This French word means the art of aging and refining cheese.

AFFINEUR/AFFINEUSE: A person who professionally ages or ripens cheese. In the American artisan world, many of the cheese-makers are also the affineur or affineuse, but in some European countries, the cheeses are picked up from the cheesemaker and then aged by an affineur or affineuse.

AGING CHEESE: This means to ripen cheese.

AGED CHEESE: Cheese that has been ripened for several months or several years, depending on the cheese and the cheese-maker.

ANNATTO: This South American seed from the achiote tree gives cheddar its orange color.

ARTISAN: This is the opposite of industrial cheese. It is cheese that is handcrafted or crafted with care.

AMERICAN ARTISAN: These are new, often original cheeses, crafted by American cheesemakers with care.

AROMA: This is the smell that comes from a cheese.

BLOOMY RIND: A cheese that has a soft, white rind like Brie is a bloomy rind.

BLUE CHEESE: Blue cheese has a mold added to create its distinctive blue or blue-green color and sharp flavors.

BOVINE GROWTH HORMONE: Bovine growth hormone, also known as soma-totropin, is a hormone that is injected into cows to make them produce more milk (it is extracted from cows' pituitary glands). It is also known as recombinant bovine growth hormone or recombinant bovine somato-tropin (rBGH or rBST). The recombinant version is a genetically engineered version that is most commonly used. Bovine growth hormone is allowed in the United States, but it is outlawed in Europe. Some studies suggest that it is hazardous to the health of humans, others say it is safe. Cows that have been injected with hormones typically have shorter milking lives than those who are milked naturally.

BRINE: A salt solution used to make some firm and hard cheeses like Emmentaler or Gouda.

BROWSERS: Animals that eat leaves, bark, twigs, shrubs, and vines, like goats, are browsers.

CASEIN: The milk protein in cheese takes its name from *caseus,* which is the Latin word for cheese.

CASEOPHILES: Caseophiles are people who love cheese.

CHEDDARING: The process of cutting, slabbing, and piling curds to press the whey out creates the cheese we call cheddar. This process was first created in England.

CHEESE HARP: A metal harp-shaped paddle strung with linear blades, it's the tool cheesemakers use to cut curds in the cheesemaking process.

CHEESECLOTH: A cotton cloth that is used to drain cheese curds.

CHEESE COURSE: When you serve a separate course within a meal that is made up of just cheese, with perhaps some bread and fruit on the side, it is called a cheese course, and it is usually served sixth out of seven courses.

CHÈVRE: In French, the word for goat is chèvre. This term also refers to the fresh cheese made from goat's milk.

COAGULATION: When milk proteins stick together to form curds, this process is called coagulation.

CREAM LINE: Milk that is not homogenized is known as cream line because there's a definitive line between the cream, which floats on top, and the milk, which is on the bottom.

CULTURES: Bacteria are used to make cheese. These bacterial cultures break the milk down into curds and whey.

CURDS: The solid or coagulated portions of milk during cheesemaking are called curds, and they are the part that is aged to become cheese. They are not cheese leftovers or bits of cheese.

CUTTING THE CURDS: After the rennet has been introduced to the milk, curds are cut to expel additional whey.

EWES: Female sheep are called ewes.

FARMSTEAD CHEESE: Cheeses made right there on the same farms where the animals are raised and milked are called farmstead cheeses.

FERMENTATION: The process in which milk becomes cheese or yogurt is called fermentation. It is the breakdown of carbohydrates in a food, which changes the original substance into something new.

FETA: A Greek sheep's milk cheese sometimes made in the United States from goat's milk or cow's milk; it is typically brined.

FIRM: A cheese that has aged for a longer period of time than semisoft is considered firm. A firm cheese harder to the touch than semisoft, but softer than hard cheese.

FRESH: A cheese that has not been aged or ripened is called fresh—like mozzarella or chèvre.

GRAZERS: Animals that primarily eat grass and clover, like cows and sheep, are grazers.

GRUYÈRE: Gruyère is a hard Swiss cow's milk cheese that traditionally was made in the Alps and is prized for its ability to melt (thus it is often used in fondues).

HARD: A cheese that is aged for a long period of time and has lost a lot of moisture is hard, and it is also hard to the touch.

HOMOGENIZED: When fats are broken down in milk so that they are evenly distributed throughout the milk, the milk is homogenized. Homogenization allows milk to have a longer shelf life, and in whole milk, the fat will not separate out and float to the top. Homogenized milk is not used in making cheese.

LACTOSE: The sugar in milk is called lactose. Bacteria eat the lactose in the formation of cheese.

LACTIC ACID: When the bacteria eat the sugars in milk during cheesemaking, lactic acid is formed.

MAÎTRE FROMAGER: In fancy restaurants, they often have a cheese expert who has studied cheese and will help you navigate a restaurant's cheese selection. They are like a sommelier for cheese.

MICROBIAL RENNET: In the past, most cheeses used rennet, an enzyme from the lining of calves' stomachs, to coagulate cheese. But today this enzyme is produced by microbes or bacteria, and it is more common than regular rennet in cheesemaking.

PASTA FILATA: Fresh mozzarella is created by this process, which involves dipping the curds into hot water, which causes the curds to release additional whey, and then the cheese is stretched and kneaded. Besides mozzarella, string, provolone, and Oaxaca cheese is made this way.

PASTE: The interior part of a cheese is called the paste.

PASTEURIZATION: Milk is heated up to high temperatures to kill germs or unwanted bacteria. There are three types of pasteurization: gentle pasteurization, in which it is heated to 145 degrees Fahrenheit for 30 minutes, then cooled; high temperature, short-time pasteurization or HTST, in which it is heated to 161 degrees Fahrenheit for 15 seconds, then cooled; and ultra-high temperature pasteurization or UHT, in which milk is heated to 200 degrees Fahrenheit for about 2 seconds, then cooled. UHT is known in most quality dairy circles as "sterilization," because it ruins the taste. UHT is used for a longer shelf life; UHT milk can actually sit on the shelf for six months or longer without refrigeration.

PLUG A CHEESE: When a judge or cheesemaker removes a sample from a wheel of cheese, they plug the cheese.

PROCESSED CHEESE: This isn't really cheese. It is a cheese product. The cheese is heat-treated and mixed with emulsifiers and other additives that keep it from breaking down when heated.

QUESO ASADERO: (KAY-so AH-sah-DAY-ro) This Hispanic-style cheese is a melting cheese.

QUESO COTIJA: (KAY-so KO-tee-ha) This Hispanic-style firm, salty cheese, is one of the aged Hispanic cheeses. It is similar to a dry feta.

QUESO BLANCO: (KAY-so BLAN-ko) This "white cheese" is the most popular cheese in Mexico and Latin America. It is a fresh cheese typically made from skimmed milk, and it is sort of like a cross between cottage cheese and mozzarella.

QUESO FRESCO: (KAY-so FRESS-ko) This Hispanic-style cheese literally means "fresh cheese" and is a white cheese, sometimes made from cow's and goat's milks combined. It is crumbly and tangy and, when heated, it will soften but not melt.

QUESO OAXACA: (KAY-so wha-HA-ka) This Hispanic-style cheese is a melting cheese, and it is often used to fill quesadillas.

QUESO PANELA: (KAY-so PAHN-ay-la) Sometimes known as *queso de canasta* or "basket cheese" because it often has an imprint of a basket on it.

RAW MILK: Unpasteurized milk is known as raw milk.

rBGH: Recombinant bovine growth hormone is a synthetically produced, genetically engineered version of the growth hormone that is injected into cows to make them produce more milk.

RENNET: The enzyme used to coagulate cheese is called rennet. It is also known as chymosin, and it used to exclusively come from the stomachs of calves, but today most rennet is produced by microbes in a laboratory.

RICOTTA: Ricotta is an Italian cheese that used to be made from the leftover whey from mozzarella production.

RIND: The outside surface of a cheese is called the rind. Some cheeses have rinds, others do not, and different rinds are developed through different methods of cheesemaking.

RIPENING: The process of aging a cheese until it is ready to be sold and eaten is called ripening or affinaging.

SALTING: Salting or adding salt to the cheese curds is always part of the cheesemaking process. Sometimes the salt is rubbed, sometimes it is mixed in with the cheese, and sometimes, wheels of cheese are floated in a saltwater solution. The salt helps stop the bacterial cultures from changing the cheese too much.

SEMISOFT: A cheese that has been aged longer than fresh cheeses but still is pliable and has enough moisture in it is called semisoft.

TERROIR: This French word explains how geography and different environments have a very distinctive effect on food products, especially cheese and wine. Artisan cheese producers often describe how their environment or *terroir* affects the taste of their cheese.

TRIER: This tool sort of looks like an apple corer, and it is used by professional cheese judges and cheesemakers to remove samples from large wheels of cheese.

TUROPHILES: Cheese lovers can be called *turophiles.*

UMAMI: Besides sweet, salty, sour, and bitter, there is a "fifth" taste called *umami.* It is sort of like a mushroom taste, and many cheeses have an *umami* flavor.

UNHOMOGENIZED: Milk that hasn't been homogenized or had its fats broken down and evenly distributed is unhomogenized. Unhomogenized milk is the type of milk used in cheesemaking.

WASHED RIND: Cheese in which the rind is washed with brine, salt, beer, wine or some other mixture to create flavors is called a washed-rind cheese. Washed-rind cheeses have very strong aromas, but their intense smells often belie mild tastes.

WHEY: When cheese is made, there is a liquid protein that is leftover, and that is called whey. It's part of what Miss Muffet was eating, and it used to be considered waste. Today, however, many cheesemakers sell their whey, which then gets incorporated into protein bars and many other foods.

INDEX